MATH Trailblazers®

A BALANCED MATHEMATICS PROGRAM INTEGRATING SCIENCE AND LANGUAGE ARTS

Unit Resource Guide
Unit 9
Grouping by Tens

THIRD EDITION

KENDALL/HUNT PUBLISHING COMPANY
4050 Westmark Drive   Dubuque, Iowa 52002

A TIMS® Curriculum
University of Illinois at Chicago

UIC The University of Illinois
at Chicago

The original edition was based on work supported by the National Science Foundation under grant
No. MDR 9050226 and the University of Illinois at Chicago. Any opinions, findings, and conclusions
or recommendations expressed in this publication are those of the author(s) and do not necessarily
reflect the views of the granting agencies.

Letter Home

Grouping by Tens

Date: _____

Dear Family Member:

In this unit, your child will continue to explore number relationships. For example, for the number 42, your child will form 4 groups of ten cubes and have two cubes left over. As a class, we will talk about the groupings as 4 tens and 2 ones. Building numbers in groups of ten helps us understand our number system.

We also will work with story problems that include addition and subtraction with multiples of ten. Solving problems in different contexts helps give meaning to mathematics.

You can provide additional support at home by doing activities such as the following:

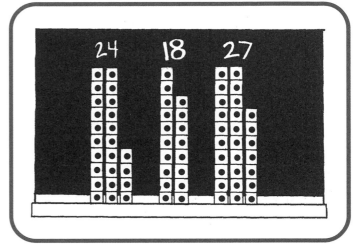

Building numbers with connecting cubes to show tens and ones

- **Buzz.** Play a variation of the game *Buzz*. Choose an even number from 2 through 8, such as 6. Players count by twos. Anytime the number has a 6 in it, the player says, "Buzz." So, the counting would go: 2, 4, BUZZ, 8 . . . 14, BUZZteen, 18, and so on. Repeat, choosing another "buzz" number.
- **Numbers in Print.** Look for numbers in print such as in the newspaper, on calendars, and on packaging. Use beans (cereal pieces, etc.) to build those numbers in groups of ten. For example, 34 is three groups of ten and four ones.
- **Spin for Beans.** During this unit, your child will play the game *Spin for Beans*. If your child brings the game home, play it together.

Thank you for your continued interest in your child's mathematics development.

Sincerely,

_____

Carta al hogar

Agrupando de a diez

Fecha: _____

Estimado miembro de familia:

En esta unidad, su hijo/a continuará explorando las relaciones entre los números. Por ejemplo, para el número 42, su hijo/a formará 4 grupos de 10 cubos y le sobrarán 2 cubos. En clase, nos referiremos a las agrupaciones como 4 decenas y 2 unidades. Construir números en grupos de diez nos ayuda a entender nuestro sistema numérico.

También trabajaremos con problemas que incluyan sumas y restas con múltiplos de diez. Resolver problemas en contextos diferentes ayuda a que las matemáticas tengan sentido.

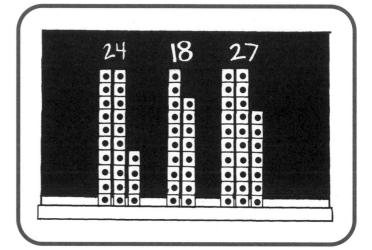

Construir números con cubos para mostrar las decenas y las unidades

Usted puede proveer apoyo adicional en casa haciendo actividades como las siguientes:

- **Paso.** Jueguen una variante del juego *"Buzz"*. Escoja un número entre el 2 y el 8, por ejemplo 6. Los jugadores cuentan de dos en dos. Cada vez que toque un número que contenga un 6, el jugador dice "Paso". Es decir que al contar se diría: 2, 4, PASO, 8...14, DieciPASO, 18, etc. Repita el juego eligiendo otros números para "pasar".

- **Números impresos.** Busque números impresos en periódicos, calendarios, y en paquetes. Use frijoles (o trocitos de cereal, etc.) para formar estos números en grupos de diez. Por ejemplo, 34 está formado por tres grupos de diez y cuatro unidades.

- **Ruleta de frijoles.** Durante esta unidad, su hijo/a tendrá la oportunidad de jugar con una *Ruleta de frijoles*. Si su hijo/a trae el juego a casa, juéguenlo juntos.

Gracias por su continuo interés en el avance de su hijo/a en matemáticas.

Atentamente,

_____

Table of Contents

Unit 9
Grouping by Tens

Outline
Grouping by Tens

Unit Summary

Estimated Class Sessions **11-12**

This unit explores number relationships and number patterns on the *100 Chart*. It extends the partitioning work begun in Unit 2 to multiples of ten. Students group and count objects by tens and ones. They compare and order two-digit numbers. The lab *Full of Beans* allows students to apply their grouping and counting skills in an investigation of volume and units.

Major Concept Focus

- grouping and counting by tens and ones
- comparing and ordering numbers
- ten frames
- multiple solution strategies
- identifying intervals
- investigating volume
- representing numbers with tens and ones
- TIMS Laboratory Method
- number patterns on the *100 Chart*
- Game: grouping and adding

Pacing Suggestions

- If your students used *Math Trailblazers*® in kindergarten, plan for the minimum number of recommended sessions for each lesson.
- Lesson 8 *Full of Beans* is a laboratory investigation. Make use of *Math Trailblazers* connections to other subjects by having students collect data during science time.

Assessment Indicators

Use the following Assessment Indicators and the *Observational Assessment Record* that follows the Background section in this unit to assess students on key ideas.

A1. Can students group and count objects by tens and ones?

A2. Can students count objects by twos, fives, and tens?

A3. Can students describe a number in relation to other numbers?

A4. Can students measure length using nonstandard units (links)?

A5. Can students make and interpret bar graphs?

A6. Can students use data to solve problems involving volume?

A7. Can students represent two-digit numbers using manipulatives, ten frames, and *100 Charts?*

Unit Planner

KEY: SG = Student Guide, AB = Adventure Book, URG = Unit Resource Guide, DPP = Daily Practice and Problems, and TIG = Teacher Implementation Guide.

	Lesson Information	**Supplies**	**Copies/Transparencies**
Lesson 1 **Spill the Beans** URG Pages 25–33 SG Page 160 DPP A–B *Estimated Class Sessions* **1-2**	**Activity** Pairs of students count 40–70 beans and then discuss grouping and counting strategies. **Math Facts Strategies** DPP item A provides subtraction facts practice. **Homework** Assign the *Group and Count* Homework Page. **Assessment** 1. As you observe groups working, note students who need supervised practice in grouping by tens to find the total. Record your observations on the *Observational Assessment Record*. 2. Have students complete a performance assessment. Create stations with set numbers of groups of objects. Assess students' abilities to group objects correctly into tens and ones. 3. Use Assessment Indicator A1 and the *Observational Assessment Record* to record students' abilities to group objects by tens and ones left over.	• 40–70 lima beans per student pair • 2-pound container of beans • small scoop	• 1 copy of *Ten Frames* URG Page 31 per student, optional • 1 copy of *Four-column Data Table* URG Page 32 per student • 1 transparency of *Four-column Data Table* URG Page 32 • 1 copy of *Observational Assessment Record* URG Pages 11–12 to be used throughout this unit
Lesson 2 **More or Less than 100?** URG Pages 34–39 SG Page 161 DPP C–D *Estimated Class Sessions* **1**	**Activity** Students make stacks of cubes to represent the number of letters in their first names; they group and count to find the class total. **Homework** Assign the *How Many Letters?* Homework Page. **Assessment** 1. Use DPP item D to assess students' abilities to write number sentences for subtraction situations. 2. Use Assessment Indicators A1 and A7 and the *Observational Assessment Record* to record students' abilities to group and count objects by tens and ones and to represent two-digit numbers using connecting cubes.	• 30 connecting cubes per student group • 1 calculator per student	
Lesson 3 **Spin for Beans** URG Pages 40–47 SG Pages 163–164 DPP E–F *Estimated Class Sessions* **1**	**Game** Students use ten frames to organize beans in a grouping and recording game. **Homework** Students play *Spin for Beans 50* with a family member at home. **Assessment** 1. As you observe children playing the game, assess the following skills: • counting by tens and ones; • naming using grouping language (e.g., 2 tens and 4 ones); • using conventional number names (e.g., 24). Use Assessment Indicator A1 and the *Observational Assessment Record* to record students' abilities with these skills. 2. Use DPP item F as an assessment.	• 1 clear plastic spinner per student pair and 1 for the teacher • 100 baby lima beans per student pair and 50 baby lima beans for the teacher	• 1 transparency of *Spin for Beans 50 Recording Sheet* URG Page 46 • 1 copy of *Spin for Beans 50 Recording Sheet* URG Page 46 per student or more as needed • 1 transparency of *Spin for Beans 50 Playing Mat* URG Page 47 • 1 copy of *Spin for Beans 50 Playing Mat* URG Page 47 per student or more as needed • 1 transparency of *Spin for Beans 50* SG Page 163

	Lesson Information	**Supplies**	**Copies/ Transparencies**

Lesson 4

The 50 Chart

URG Pages 48–56
SG Page 165
DPP G–H

Estimated Class Sessions

1

Activity
Students build cube trains of tens and ones, place them on the *50 Chart*, and identify number patterns to fill in the missing numbers in the chart.

Math Facts Strategies
DPP items G and H provide practice with addition and subtraction facts strategies.

Assessment
Use Assessment Indicator A3 and the *Observational Assessment Record* to record students' abilities to describe a number in relation to other numbers.

- 50 connecting cubes per student pair
- index card with the number 32
- 50 overhead colored tiles, optional

- 1 copy of *Find the Numbers* URG Page 55 per student pair
- 1 transparency of *50 Chart* SG Page 165

Lesson 5

The 100 Chart

URG Pages 57–69
SG Pages 167–169
DPP I–L

Estimated Class Sessions

2

Activity
Students explore patterns on the *100 Chart.*

Math Facts Strategies
Item L provides practice with subtraction facts strategies.

Homework
Students complete *Counting by Tens* Homework Page at home after completing the first column in class.

Assessment
1. Make additional copies of the *Target Numbers* Blackline Master and give students a new set of numbers to fill in the center boxes of the five-square segments. Ask them to fill in the blank boxes as before.
2. Use Assessment Indicators A2, A3, and A7 and the *Observational Assessment Record* to record students' abilities to count by twos, fives, and tens, to describe a number in relation to other numbers, and to represent two-digit numbers using *100 Charts.*

- 100 connecting cubes grouped in tens per student pair
- overhead color tiles, optional

- 2 copies of *Target Numbers* URG Page 65 per student
- 1 copy of *Tricky Target Numbers* URG Page 66 per student, optional
- 1 copy of *Desk-Size 100 Chart* URG Page 67 per student, optional
- 1 transparency of *100 Chart* SG Page 167

Lesson 6

Measuring with Connecting Links

URG Pages 70–76
SG Page 171
DPP M–N

Estimated Class Sessions

1

Activity
Students measure classroom objects with chain links, place the measurement numbers in intervals of 20, and check for reasonableness.

Homework
Students play *Guess My Number* at home.

Assessment
Use Assessment Indicator A4 and the *Observational Assessment Record* to record students' abilities to measure length in nonstandard units.

- 2 index cards per student pair and 15 index cards for the extension
- 100 connecting links in different colored 10-link chains per student pair
- masking tape
- easel paper, optional

- 1 copy of *Desk-Size 100 Chart* URG Page 67 per student
- 1 copy of *100 Chart* URG Page 76 per student, optional

(Continued)

	Lesson Information	Supplies	Copies/Transparencies

Lesson 7

Numbers in the News

URG Pages 77–84
SG Pages 173–174
DPP O–P

Estimated Class Sessions
1

Activity
Students explore multiple relationships among two-digit numbers.

Homework
Assign the *Find Numbers in the News* Homework Pages.

Assessment
1. Use the Journal Prompt as an assessment.
2. Use Assessment Indicator A3 and the *Observational Assessment Record* to record students' abilities to describe a number in relation to other numbers.

• 1 piece of easel paper per student pair and some for the teacher
• 1 newspaper headline per student pair
• old newspapers, optional
• 100 connecting cubes per student pair, optional
• scissors

• 1 headline from *Numbers in the News* URG Page 83 per student pair, optional
• 1 copy of *Desk-Size 100 Chart* URG Page 67 per student, optional

Lesson 8

Full of Beans

URG Pages 85–92
SG Pages 175–179
DPP Q–V

Estimated Class Sessions
3

Lab
Students apply their grouping and counting skills in an investigation of volume and units.

Assessment
1. Use the *Maria and José's Graph* Assessment Page.
2. Fill a small container with a group of objects and another identical container with a group of larger objects. Label one jar A and the other B. Ask students to estimate how many objects are in each container and record their estimates and reasoning in their journals.
3. Use DPP item S as a short assessment.
4. Use Assessment Indicators A5 and A6 and the *Observational Assessment Record* to document students' abilities to make and interpret bar graphs and to use data to solve problems involving volume.
5. Transfer appropriate documentation from the Unit 9 *Observational Assessment Record* to students' *Individual Assessment Record Sheets*.

• enough large beans (kidney) to fill a two-ounce cup (approximately 40 beans) per student pair
• enough small beans (large lima) to fill a two-ounce cup (approximately 80 beans) per student pair
• 2 two-ounce cups per student pair
• 1 modified egg carton or 2 copies of *Ten Frames* URG Page 31 per student pair
• 2 large containers
• 2 same-size jars: one filled with small objects and one filled with similar, but larger objects

• 1 transparency of *Full of Beans* SG Pages 175–178
• 1 copy of *Individual Assessment Record Sheet* TIG Assessment section per student, previously copied for use throughout the year

Preparing for Upcoming Lessons

Place square-inch tiles in a learning center for students to explore prior to beginning Unit 10.

A current list of literature and software connections is available at *www.mathtrailblazers.com.* You can also find information on connections in the *Teacher Implementation Guide* Literature List and Software List sections.

Literature Connections

Suggested Titles

- Sloat, Teri. *From One to One Hundred.* Puffin Books, New York, 1991.

Software Connections

- *Kid Pix* helps students draw, write, and illustrate math concepts.
- *Math Concepts One . . . Two . . . Three!* provides practice with counting, estimation, comparing and ordering numbers, as well as estimating and measuring time, money, length, temperature, and mass.
- *Mighty Math Carnival Countdown* provides practice with place value concepts, basic operations (addition and subtraction), and developing the concept of equals and more and less with numbers up to 1000.
- *Mighty Math Zoo Zillions* provides practice with basic operations (adding and subtracting), rounding, skip counting, and identifying even and odd numbers.
- *Tenth Network: Grouping and Place Value* practices grouping objects by twos, fives, and tens.

Teaching All Math Trailblazers Students

Math Trailblazers lessons are designed for students with a wide range of abilities. The lessons are flexible and do not require significant adaptation for diverse learning styles or academic levels. However, when needed, lessons can be tailored to allow students to engage their abilities to the greatest extent possible while building knowledge and skills.

To assist you in meeting the needs of all students in your classroom, this section contains information about some of the features in the curriculum that allow all students access to mathematics. For additional information, see the Teaching the *Math Trailblazers* Student: Meeting Individual Needs section in the *Teacher Implementation Guide*.

Differentiation Opportunities in this Unit

Games

Use games to promote or extend understanding of math concepts and to practice skills with children who need more practice.

- *Spin for Beans 50* from Lesson 3 *Spin for Beans*
- *Guess My Number* from Lesson 6 *Measuring with Connecting Links*

Laboratory Experiments

Laboratory experiments enable students to solve problems using a variety of representations including pictures, tables, graphs, and symbols. Teachers can assign or adapt parts of the analysis according to the student's ability. The following lesson is a lab:

- Lesson 8 *Full of Beans*

Journal Prompts

Journal prompts provide opportunities for students to explain and reflect on mathematical problems. They can help both students who need practice explaining their ideas and students who benefit from answering higher order questions. Students with various learning styles can express themselves using pictures, words, and sentences. Teachers can alter journal prompts to suit students' ability levels. The following lessons contain a journal prompt:

- Lesson 7 *Numbers in the News*
- Lesson 8 *Full of Beans*

Extensions

Use extensions to enrich lessons. Many extensions provide opportunities to further involve or challenge students of all abilities. Take a moment to review the extensions prior to beginning this unit. Some extensions may require additional preparation and planning. The following lessons contain extensions:

- Lesson 1 *Spill the Beans*
- Lesson 5 *The 100 Chart*
- Lesson 6 *Measuring with Connecting Links*
- Lesson 8 *Full of Beans*

Background
Grouping by Tens

This unit begins by investigating two major place value ideas:

- Grouping objects by tens to count them (e.g., 4 groups of ten and 2 ones left over); and

- Using language to make connections among groupings of tens and ones (4 tens and 2 ones), their names (forty-two), and standard symbols (42).

The first three lessons focus on this content to build understanding of our place value system. In Lesson 3 *Spin for Beans,* students make the transition from calling the ungrouped counters "leftovers" to calling them "ones."

Lessons 4 and 5 help students recognize the connection between tens and ones and the sequence of whole numbers to 100. The *50 Chart* and the *100 Chart* illustrate the connection between, for example, the number 34 and groups of 3 tens and 4 ones. Students discuss emerging place value patterns.

In Lessons 6 and 7, students use their work with tens and ones to begin an examination of number relationships.

Lesson 8 *Full of Beans* is a lab in which students explore volume by filling containers with nonstandard units. The investigation enables students to apply their knowledge of grouping by tens while building concepts of volume. In particular, students investigate the inverse relationship between the size of the unit and the measurement of the volume.

Throughout the unit, children build number sense by exploring relationships among numbers and the relative size of numbers.

Resources

- Carpenter, T.P., D.A. Carey & V.L. Kouba. "A Problem-Solving Approach to the Operations" in J.N. Payne (Ed.), *Mathematics for the Young Child.* National Council of Teachers of Mathematics, Reston, VA, 1990.

- Carpenter, T.P., & J.M. Moser. "The Acquisition of Addition and Subtraction Concepts in Grades One through Three" in *Journal for Research in Mathematics Education,* 15 (3), 1984.

Observational Assessment Record

A1 Can students group and count objects by tens and ones?

A2 Can students count objects by twos, fives, and tens?

A3 Can students describe a number in relation to other numbers?

A4 Can students measure length using nonstandard units (links)?

A5 Can students make and interpret bar graphs?

A6 Can students use data to solve problems involving volume?

A7 Can students represent two-digit numbers using manipulatives, ten frames, and *100 Charts*?

A8 _____

Name	A1	A2	A3	A4	A5	A6	A7	A8	Comments
1.									
2.									
3.									
4.									
5.									
6.									
7.									
8.									
9.									
10.									
11.									
12.									
13.									

Name	A1	A2	A3	A4	A5	A6	A7	A8	Comments
14.									
15.									
16.									
17.									
18.									
19.									
20.									
21.									
22.									
23.									
24.									
25.									
26.									
27.									
28.									
29.									
30.									
31.									
32.									

Unit 9

Daily Practice and Problems
Grouping by Tens

A DPP Menu for Unit 9

Two Daily Practice and Problems (DPP) items are included for each class session listed in the Unit Outline. A scope and sequence chart for the DPP is in the *Teacher Implementation Guide*.

Icons in the Teacher Notes column designate the subject matter of each DPP item. Each item falls into one or more of the categories listed below. A menu of the DPP items for Unit 9 follows.

N Number Sense	✖ Computation	⧗ Time	⬨ Geometry
D–F, J, K, M–V	A–D, G, I, K, L, P	C	J
7+3 Math Facts Strategies	$ Money	✎ Measurement	Data
A, G, H, L	B, F	T, V	I, K

Unit 9 Daily Practice and Problems

Students may solve the items individually, in groups, or as a class. The items may also be assigned for homework. The DPPs are also available on the Teacher Resource CD.

Student Questions	Teacher Notes
A Subtraction Facts 1 A. $7 - 2 =$ B. $10 - 3 =$ C. $25 - 5 =$	Encourage students to work individually to solve each problem. Then, ask students to share their methods, discussing the various strategies they used. For example, to solve A and B some students may count back. A. 5 B. 7 C. 20
B Who Has More? Jim has 5 dimes. Bob has 1 quarter, 1 dime, and 2 nickels. Who has more money?	Jim with 50¢ has more money than Bob with 45¢. Use overhead coins or pictures to illustrate the problem.
C What Day of the Week? 1. September 17, 2002, was a Tuesday. What day of the week was September 19? 2. October 2, 2002, was a Wednesday. What day of the week was October 9?	1. Thursday 2. Wednesday

D · How Many in the Bag?

N ✖

I have _____ beans in the bag. Now I am taking out _____ beans. How many beans are left in the bag?

Write a number sentence that describes my bag now.

Place an appropriate number of beans (10–20) in the bag. Take out several beans to create a subtraction situation. For example, place 15 beans in the bag. Remove 5 beans. Ask students how many are left. An appropriate number sentence for this example is $15 - 5 = 10$. Students were introduced to this activity in Unit 8 Lesson 4 *How Many in the Bag?*

E · Making a Link Chain

N

Make a 27-link chain. Each group of ten links should be the same color. Make the leftover links all one color as well.

A 27-link chain is made up of _____ groups of ten and _____ leftovers.

2, 7; repeat with link chains of various lengths.

F · Groups of 10 and Leftovers

$ N

1. Rami has 32 pennies. If she puts them in groups of ten, she will have _____ groups of ten and _____ leftovers.

2. T.J. had a pile of pennies. To count them, he made groups of ten. If T.J. has 4 groups of ten and 6 leftover pennies, how many pennies does he have in all?

Counters such as beans or cubes should be available to students.

1. 3 groups of ten and 2 leftovers

2. 46 pennies

G Subtraction Facts 2

A. $8 - 6 =$

B. $9 - 4 =$

C. $32 - 3 =$

Encourage students to work individually to solve each problem. Then, ask students to share their methods, discussing their various strategies. For example, for A some students may suggest counting up. Counting back may be used for C.

A. 2

B. 5

C. 29

H At the Circus

1. Todd counted 3 acrobats riding unicycles. Six acrobats were swinging on the trapeze. How many acrobats were performing at once?

2. Gwen counted 4 elephants in the first ring at the circus. She counted 5 in the second ring. There were 3 in the third ring. How many elephants were there altogether?

Encourage students to write number sentences for their problems.

1. 9 acrobats

2. 12 elephants

Number of Letters

Joseph made this table for the names of his family members.

First Name	Number of Letters
Joseph	6
May	3
Elizabeth	9
Charlie	7

1. What is the total number of letters Joseph recorded for his family?

2. Which name has the most letters?

3. Which name has the least letters?

4. How many more letters are in the longest name than in the shortest name?

1. 25 letters

2. Elizabeth

3. May

4. 6 letters

J **Patterns**

Write A, B, or C under each object to show the pattern. Circle the repeating pattern unit.

1. △△◯△△◯△△◯

2. ▯▯▢▢◯◯▯▯▢

1. AABAABAAB; AAB is the pattern unit to be circled.

2. AABBCCAAB; AABBCC is the pattern unit to be circled.

K **Names and Letters**

In Miss White's class, five students reported the total number of letters in the names they collected.

Sally's family: 32 letters
Roberto's gerbil family: 12 letters
Mary's family: 28 letters
Sam's family: 15 letters
Joseph's family: 25 letters

1. Predict whether these five students will have more or less than 100 letters total.

2. Use a calculator to check your prediction. List the keys you pressed on the calculator to get your answer.

1. Encourage students to explain how they decided on their prediction.

2. 112; Students may press:
   32 + 12 + 28 + 15 + 25 =

L Subtraction Facts 3

A. $6 - 3 =$

B. $11 - 5 =$

C. $27 - 4 =$

Encourage students to work individually to solve each problem. Then, ask students to share their methods, discussing the various strategies they used. Some students may use doubles to solve A and B.

  A. 3

  B. 6

  C. 23

M 100 Chart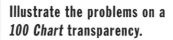

1. What number is above 14 on the *100 Chart?*

2. What number is below 14 on the *100 Chart?*

3. What number is to the right of 14? to the left?

4. I am on 14. I move 3 spaces to the right. What number do I land on?

5. I am on 14. I move 3 spaces to the left. What number do I land on?

Illustrate the problems on a *100 Chart* transparency.

  1. 4

  2. 24

  3. 15; 13

  4. 17

  5. 11

I'm Thinking of a Number

What number am I thinking of?

1. I am thinking of a number that is 2 tens and 3 ones.

2. I am thinking of a number that is 2 more than 17.

3. I am thinking of a number that is 4 more than 28.

4. I am thinking of a number that is 3 less than 75.

5. I am thinking of a number that is 6 less than 43.

6. I am thinking of a number that is 10 more than 67.

Students may use their *100 Charts* to help them solve these riddles.

1. 23

2. 19

3. 32

4. 72

5. 37

6. 77

Student Questions	Teacher Notes

 Skip Counting on the Calculator

1. Press 1 + 5 = on your calculator.

2. Circle the answer on the *100 Chart.*

3. Continue to press the equal sign and circle each result on the chart until no more numbers can be circled.

4. Describe the patterns you see.

This item is suggested for calculators that have a constant feature. If you press: 1 + 5 = = = = = on a calculator with a constant feature, the constant number (5) and the constant operation (addition) will be repeated each time = is pressed. Keystrokes may vary for different calculators.

Display a transparency of a *100 Chart.* After you press 1 + 5 =, ask a student to circle the result on the transparency. Continue to ask volunteers to circle the new result each time = is pressed.

P Spin for Beans 50

Spin for Beans was introduced in Lesson 3. Illustrate with a *100 Chart* or *Ten Frames* transparency.

1. Marissa and Tyrone are playing *Spin for Beans 50.* Marissa has 4 full ten frames and 6 leftovers. Tyrone has 3 full frames and 9 leftovers. Who is winning?

1. Marissa

2. 4 beans

3. 11 beans

2. How many more beans does Marissa need to reach 50?

3. How many more beans does Tyrone need to reach 50?

Guess My Number

I am thinking of a number. Guess what it is. After each guess I will tell you whether you should guess higher or lower.

The first time you play, start with a small range of numbers such as 1–20. Gradually increase the range to 1–30, 1–40, etc., until students are comfortable guessing a number between 1–100. Students may use their *100 Charts*. Students play a version of this game in Lesson 6 *Measuring with Connecting Links*.

 Skip Counting from Zero

1. If we skip count by twos, will we reach 47? 58?

Students use a calculator and a *100 Chart* to reinforce the patterns.

1. We won't reach 47, but we will reach 58.

2. We will reach 45, but we won't reach 54.

3. We will reach 100, but we won't reach 11.

2. If we skip count by fives, will we reach 45? 54?

3. If we skip count by tens, will we reach 100? 11?

Student Questions	Teacher Notes

 Naming Numbers

1. Name a number between 40 and 50.

2. Name a number between 40 and 50 that is closer to 40 than 50.

3. Name a number halfway between 40 and 50.

4. Name a number more than 50.

5. Name a number less than 40.

1. 41, 42, 43, 44, 45, 46, 47, 48, or 49

2. 41, 42, 43, or 44

3. 45

4. 51 or above

5. 39 or lower

 Measuring with Links

Rita measured the width of a bookcase with her 80-link chain. She reported that the bookcase was 2 groups of ten links and 1 more link wide.

Nick measured the width of a window. He reported that the window was 19 links wide.

Which object is wider?

Students may need links to visualize the answer. The bookcase is wider.

Target Numbers

1.
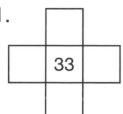
33

2.
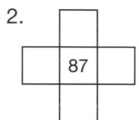
87

3.
12

Lesson 5 introduced target numbers.

1.
```
        23
   32   33   34
        43
```

2.
```
             77
   86   87   88
             97
```

3.
```
         2
   11   12   13
        22
```

 Golf Balls or Marbles?

Marge's two containers have the same volume and shape. She filled one with golf balls and the other with marbles. Which object do you think there are more of?

Students may reason that since marbles are smaller than golf balls, the container will hold more marbles.

Spill the Beans

Lesson Overview

Estimated Class Sessions

1-2

Children group and count a small collection of beans by tens and ones left over. This experience reinforces the idea that grouping objects before counting them is more efficient and accurate than counting by ones.

Key Content

- Grouping and counting objects by tens and ones left over.
- Representing two-digit numbers using grouping language (e.g., 2 tens and 3 ones left over) and conventional names (e.g., 23).

Math Facts Strategies

DPP item A provides practice with subtraction facts.

Homework

Assign the *Group and Count* Homework Page.

Assessment

1. As you observe groups working, note students who need supervised practice in grouping by tens to find the total. Record your observations on the *Observational Assessment Record*.
2. Have students complete a performance assessment. Create stations with set numbers of groups of objects. Assess students' abilities to group objects correctly into tens and ones.
3. Use Assessment Indicator A1 and the *Observational Assessment Record* to record students' abilities to group objects by tens and ones left over.

Curriculum Sequence

Grouping by Tens

In Units 1 through 8, students encountered two-digit numbers in various contexts such as computation and measurement. In many activities, students used the language of tens and ones to describe and interpret numbers.

Grouping by Tens

Unit 11 and Unit 17 continue to investigate place value patterns in two- and three-digit numbers while helping students synthesize and extend concepts of large numbers.

Materials List

Supplies and Copies

Student	Teacher
Supplies for Each Student Pair • 40–70 lima beans	**Supplies** • 2-pound container of beans • small scoop
Copies • 1 copy of *Ten Frames* per student, optional (*Unit Resource Guide* Page 31) • 1 copy of *Four-column Data Table* per student (*Unit Resource Guide* Page 32)	**Copies/Transparencies** • 1 transparency of *Four-column Data Table* (*Unit Resource Guide* Page 32) • 1 copy of *Observational Assessment Record* to be used throughout this unit (*Unit Resource Guide* Pages 11–12)

All blackline masters including assessment, transparency, and DPP masters are also on the Teacher Resource CD.

Student Books
Group and Count (*Student Guide* Page 160)

Daily Practice and Problems
DPP items A–B (*Unit Resource Guide* Page 14)

Assessment Tools
Observational Assessment Record (*Unit Resource Guide* Pages 11–12)

Daily Practice and Problems

Suggestions for using the DPPs are on page 29.

A. Subtraction Facts 1 (URG p. 14) A. $7 - 2 =$ B. $10 - 3 =$ C. $25 - 5 =$	**B. Who Has More?** (URG p. 14) Jim has 5 dimes. Bob has 1 quarter, 1 dime, and 2 nickels. Who has more money?

Test your scoop before beginning the activity. Use a scoop that holds an appropriate number of beans for your students to count.

Teaching the Activity

Scoop and pour 40 to 70 beans on a piece of paper for each pair of students. Ask each pair to count the number of beans in their pile. Label the *Four-column Data Table* transparency with the headings shown in Figure 1. Ask students to copy your headings and record the number of beans in their pile in the fourth column on their *Four-column Data Table.* Record each number on the transparency as pairs report their totals.

Ask students to explain how they counted their beans and what problems they had, if any, in counting them. Most students will have counted by ones although a few pairs may have grouped and counted by twos, fives, or tens. It is expected that some pairs will have had problems organizing and counting the beans. Ask students whether their counting experiences were easy or difficult and why.

If no students used the strategy of counting by tens, remind the class of previous experiences in which they grouped and counted by tens (for example, Unit 5 *Grouping and Counting*). If some students used this strategy, encourage them to discuss how it was helpful. Emphasize that counting by tens is one efficient way to count. Follow up the discussion by asking all pairs to group their beans by tens. Have each pair report the total number of groups of ten and the number of leftovers. Record their answers on the transparency as shown in Figure 1.

Object	Number of Groups of 10	Number of Leftovers	Number
beans	4	3	43

Figure 1: *Groups of tens and ones for 43 beans*

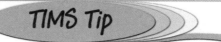

TIMS Tip

If students have difficulty forming groups of tens, you might have them use ten frames.

Explain that 43 is 4 groups of ten and 3 leftovers. Use other examples of students' totals to emphasize this idea. If students are slow to grasp this grouping concept, they will have several additional experiences in this and later units to reinforce the connection among grouping, names, and standard symbols. It is appropriate to keep the discussion simple and informal at this stage.

Each pair of students should repeat the activity several times with new scoops of beans as time allows.

Math Facts Strategies

DPP item A provides practice with subtraction facts.

Homework and Practice

- Assign the *Group and Count* Homework Page and have students bring it to class by the day indicated on the sheet. Discuss students' counting experiences when they return their homework. Invite them to tell what they counted and to share problems or successes they may have had.

- DPP item B practices counting and comparing money.

Assessment

- As you observe groups working, note students who need supervised practice in grouping by tens to find the total. Record your observations on the *Observational Assessment Record*.

- Ask your students to complete a performance assessment. Create stations with set numbers of groups of objects. You might use paper clips, beads, or links. Direct students to group these objects into tens and ones and record their count on a *Four-column Data Table*. Assess students' abilities to group objects correctly into tens and ones by collecting and reviewing their data tables. Use the *Observational Assessment Record* to document students' abilities to represent numbers using objects grouped by tens and ones.

Extension

As students count their collections of beans, ask them to identify which totals are between 40 and 50, 50 and 60, and so on.

Name _____ Date _____

Group and Count

Homework

Dear Family Member:

In class, we are counting by grouping objects in tens and leftover ones. You can help provide additional practice for your child by gathering a collection of objects and setting it out for your child to group and count. Change the total number of objects at least two times. Some ideas for objects to use are cereal pieces, nuts, pasta, raisins, pennies, buttons, and marbles. There should be 40–70 objects each time your child groups and counts.

Thank you for your cooperation.

Find objects to count. Ask an adult or an older sister or brother to help you.

Object	Number of Groups of 10	Number of Leftovers	Number

Return this paper on _____.

160   SG • Grade 1 • Unit 9 • Lesson 1   Spill the Beans

Student Guide - page 160 (Answers on p. 33)

At a Glance

Math Facts Strategies and Daily Practice and Problems

DPP item A provides practice with subtraction facts. Item B compares two quantities of money.

Teaching the Activity

1. Give each student pair a scoop of beans to count.
2. Students count and record the number of beans on the *Four-column Data Table*.
3. Students discuss how they counted the beans.
4. Students group their beans into piles of tens and ones left over, then record their observations on the *Four-column Data Table*.
5. Students count and record additional collections of beans as time allows.

Homework

Assign the *Group and Count* Homework Page.

Assessment

1. As you observe groups working, note students who need supervised practice in grouping by tens to find the total. Record your observations on the *Observational Assessment Record*.
2. Have students complete a performance assessment. Create stations with set numbers of groups of objects. Assess students' abilities to group objects correctly into tens and ones.
3. Use Assessment Indicator A1 and the *Observational Assessment Record* to record students' abilities to group objects by tens and ones left over.

Extension

Have students identify which bean totals are between 40 and 50, 50 and 60, and so on.

Answer Key is on page 33.

Notes:

Ten Frames

Name _____ Date _____

_____

Four-column Data Table, Blackline Master

Student Guide (p. 160)

Group and Count

Answers will vary.

Name _____ Date _____

Group and Count

Homework

Dear Family Member:

In class, we are counting by grouping objects in tens and leftover ones. You can help provide additional practice for your child by gathering a collection of objects and setting it out for your child to group and count. Change the total number of objects at least two times. Some ideas for objects to use are cereal pieces, nuts, pasta, raisins, pennies, buttons, and marbles. There should be 40–70 objects each time your child groups and counts.

Thank you for your cooperation.

Find objects to count. Ask an adult or an older sister or brother to help you.

Object	Number of Groups of 10	Number of Leftovers	Number

Return this paper on _____.

160 SG • Grade 1 • Unit 9 • Lesson 1   Spill the Beans

Student Guide - page 160

Lesson 2

More or Less than 100?

Estimated Class Sessions

1

Lesson Overview

This activity continues the focus on grouping and naming experiences, emphasizing the idea that 100 represents 10 tens. Children predict the total number of letters in the first names of all the students in the class and then use connecting cubes to determine whether the total is more or less than 100.

Key Content

- Connecting mathematics to real-world situations: predicting the total number of letters in first names in the class.
- Grouping and counting objects by tens and ones left over.
- Representing 100 as 10 tens.
- Representing two- and three-digit numbers using connecting cubes.
- Communicating mathematics orally and in writing.

Homework

Assign the *How Many Letters?* Homework Page.

Assessment

1. Use DPP item D to assess students' abilities to write number sentences for subtraction situations.
2. Use Assessment Indicators A1 and A7 and the *Observational Assessment Record* to record students' abilities to group and count objects by tens and ones and to represent two-digit numbers using connecting cubes.

Materials List

Supplies and Copies

Student	Teacher
Supplies for Each Student Group • 30 connecting cubes **Supplies for Each Student** • calculator	**Supplies**
Copies	**Copies/Transparencies**

All blackline masters including assessment, transparency, and DPP masters are also on the Teacher Resource CD.

Student Books
How Many Letters? (*Student Guide* Page 161)

Daily Practice and Problems
DPP items C–D (*Unit Resource Guide* Pages 14–15)

Assessment Tools
Observational Assessment Record (*Unit Resource Guide* Pages 11–12)

Daily Practice and Problems

Suggestions for using the DPPs are on page 37.

C. What Day of the Week? (URG p. 14)

1. September 17, 2002, was a Tuesday.
   What day of the week was September 19?
2. October 2, 2002, was a Wednesday.
   What day of the week was October 9?

D. How Many in the Bag? (URG p. 15)

I have _____ beans in the bag. Now I am taking out _____ beans. How many beans are left in the bag?

Write a number sentence that describes my bag now.

Ask students to count the letters in their first names. For example, Anna has four letters in her first name. Have volunteers share their numbers with the class. Ask:

- *Do you think the total number of letters in the first names of everyone in this class is more than 100 or less than 100?*

Students may share their predictions with the class and explain how they made their predictions.

Assign students to groups of four. Ask each student to stack cubes to show the number of letters in his or her name. Have them compare the heights of their stacks within their groups. When everyone is ready, ask students to think of some sentences that describe the number of letters in their groups. Help them get started by giving examples such as the following:

- The greatest number of letters is _____.

- The smallest number of letters is_____.

- _____ names have six letters.

- We all have the same number of letters. We each have _____ letters in our names.

Encourage students to think of their own sentences and then share them with the class.

Now, ask each group to combine the stacks for all their names into stacks of ten cubes and a stack of leftover ones. Write an example such as the one shown in Figure 2, and ask each group to report their results in the same way. Remind students that they did this in the last lesson.

2 tens and 4 ones left over   24 letters

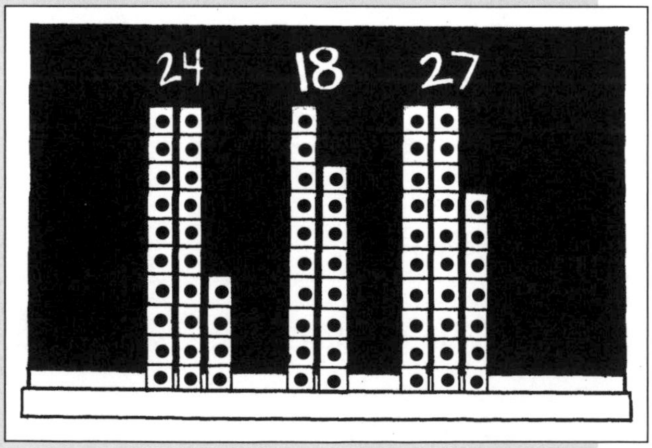

Ask each group to report their total number of letters so you can record the results on the board. Have students set the stacks of ten cubes and leftover cubes on the tray below their number as they share their results.

Explain:

- *We want to find the total number of letters for the whole class. Does anyone have ideas about how to do this?*

Guide students to the idea of counting all the group stacks on the tray. Have volunteers help combine the stacks of tens and ones and make an additional stack of the leftover cubes. Point out that it takes 10 tens to

Figure 2: *Tens and ones stacked on the board tray*

make 100, which can be verified by counting the stacks by tens. Count the total number of cubes, and have children tell whether the number is more or less than 100. To check the result, have students use calculators to add the numbers gathered from each group to get a grand total of letters in the names of everyone in the class.

Conclude the activity by asking students to compare their original predictions with the actual number. You may ask them to record the final result in their journals and write down any new ideas they might have about the activity.

Homework and Practice

- Have students complete the *How Many Letters?* Homework Page. Tell students to use the data table to record the first names and number of letters of four people or pets at home. After students hand in their homework, tell the class how many students turned in data, and then ask them to predict the total number of letters from all the homework pages. Ask, *"Would the number be about 100, 200, 300, 400?"* Make this discussion a playful encounter with larger numbers. Conclude by having students use their calculators to find the total number of letters in the homework pages.
- DPP item C practices identifying days of the week.

Assessment

- Use the *Observational Assessment Record* to document students' abilities to represent numbers using connecting cubes grouped by tens and ones.
- Use DPP item D *How Many in the Bag?* as a short assessment of students' abilities to write number sentences for subtraction situations.

Name _____ Date _____

How Many Letters?

Homework

Write the first names of four people or pets at home. Write the number of letters in each name.

First Name	Number of Letters

Total Number of Letters = _____

Draw a picture or tell how you found the total number of letters.

Return this sheet to school by _____.

More or Less than 100   SG • Grade 1 • Unit 9 • Lesson 2   161

Student Guide - page 161 *(Answers on p. 39)*

At a Glance

Math Facts Strategies and Daily Practice and Problems

DPP item C reviews the days of the week.

Teaching the Activity (A1) (A2) (A7)

1. Each student figures out how many letters are in his or her first name.
2. Students predict the total number of letters in the first names of everyone in the class.
3. In groups of four, each student makes a stack of cubes to show the number of letters in his or her name. Group members compare the heights of their stacks.
4. Students combine stacks into groups of ten cubes and a stack of leftover ones.
5. Each group reports their total number of letters and sets its stacks of cubes on the tray under their total.
6. In a whole-class discussion, students decide how they will find the total number of letters for their class.
7. The stacks of cubes for the different groups are reorganized into groups of hundreds, tens, and leftovers.
8. To conclude this lesson, students compare their predictions to the actual results.

Homework

Assign the *How Many Letters?* Homework Page.

Assessment

1. Use DPP item D to assess students' abilities to write number sentences for subtraction situations.
2. Use Assessment Indicators A1 and A7 and the *Observational Assessment Record* to record students' abilities to group and count objects by tens and ones and to represent two-digit numbers using connecting cubes.

Answer Key is on page 39.

Notes:

Student Guide (p. 161)

How Many Letters?

Answers will vary.*

Name _____ Date _____

How Many Letters?

Homework

Write the first names of four people or pets at home. Write the number of letters in each name.

First Name	Number of Letters

Total Number of Letters = _____

Draw a picture or tell how you found the total number of letters.

Return this sheet to school by _____.

More or Less than 100   SG • Grade 1 • Unit 9 • Lesson 2   161

Student Guide - page 161

---

*Answers and/or discussion are included in the Lesson Guide.

Spin for Beans

Lesson Overview

Estimated Class Sessions

1

Students practice counting objects using tens and ones. Students play *Spin for Beans* independently, in pairs, or in small groups. Players take turns spinning a spinner to determine the number of beans to take from the central pile. The goal is to be the first to accumulate 50 beans. Each player uses a ten frame to keep an ongoing record of the number of beans collected. Using ten frames provides a visual representation of two-digit numbers and grouping by tens.

Key Content

- Grouping and counting objects by tens and ones.
- Representing two-digit numbers using grouping language (e.g., 4 tens and 3 ones) and conventional names (e.g., 43).
- Representing quantities to 50 using ten frames.
- Communicating mathematics verbally and in writing.

Homework

Students play *Spin for Beans 50* with a family member at home.

Assessment

1. As you observe children playing the game, assess the following skills:
   - counting by tens and ones;
   - naming using grouping language (e.g., 2 tens and 4 ones);
   - using conventional number names (e.g., 24).
   Use Assessment Indicator A1 and the *Observational Assessment Record* to record students' abilities with these skills.
2. Use DPP item F as an assessment.

Materials List

Supplies and Copies

Student	Teacher
Supplies for Each Student Pair	**Supplies**
• 100 baby lima beans (you can substitute pennies or other small counters for the beans) • clear plastic spinner	• 50 baby lima beans (you can substitute pennies or other small counters for the beans) • clear plastic spinner
Copies	**Copies/Transparencies**
• 1 copy of *Spin for Beans 50 Recording Sheet* per student or more as needed (*Unit Resource Guide* Page 46) • 1 copy of *Spin for Beans 50 Playing Mat* per student or more as needed (*Unit Resource Guide* Page 47)	• 1 transparency of *Spin for Beans 50* (*Student Guide* Page 163) • 1 transparency of *Spin for Beans 50 Recording Sheet* (*Unit Resource Guide* Page 46) • 1 transparency of *Spin for Beans 50 Playing Mat* (*Unit Resource Guide* Page 47)

All blackline masters including assessment, transparency, and DPP masters are also on the Teacher Resource CD.

Student Books
Spin for Beans 50 (*Student Guide* Page 163)
Spin for Beans at Home (*Student Guide* Page 164)

Daily Practice and Problems
DPP items E–F (*Unit Resource Guide* Page 15)

Assessment Tools
Observational Assessment Record (*Unit Resource Guide* Pages 11–12)

E. Making a Link Chain (URG p. 15)

Make a 27-link chain. Each group of ten links should be the same color. Make the leftover links all one color as well.

A 27-link chain is made up of _____ groups of ten and _____ leftovers.

F. Groups of 10 and Leftovers
(URG p. 15)

1. Rami has 32 pennies. If she puts them in groups of ten, she will have _____ groups of ten and _____ leftovers.

2. T.J. had a pile of pennies. To count them, he made groups of ten. If T.J. has 4 groups of ten and 6 leftover pennies, how many pennies does he have in all?

Before the Game

Students will need the *Spin for Beans 50* Game Page from the *Student Guide* and one or two copies each of the *Spin for Beans 50 Recording Sheet* Blackline Master and the *Spin for Beans 50 Playing Mat* Blackline Master. Students can play two games using one playing mat and one recording sheet. Give students more copies if you want them to play more games. If students do not have enough room on their desks for all three pages, cut the playing mats and recording sheets in half lengthwise as indicated on the blackline masters.

Teaching the Game

Tell student pairs they are going to play *Spin for Beans 50*. Introduce the game by showing the transparency of the *Spin for Beans 50* Game Page and reviewing the directions with the class. Then, demonstrate the game with a student volunteer. Display the transparency of the *Spin for Beans 50 Playing Mat*. Demonstrate how to place beans for each spin on the mat and to record the number of beans each player has on the recording sheet. Figure 3 shows an example for two spins.

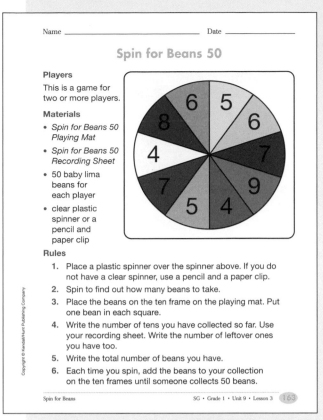

Student Guide - page 163

First spin is 7. Place 7 beans on the first ten frame. Fill in the spaces on the ten frame from left to right. Record the number of tens and ones on the recording sheet as shown below.

Second spin is 8. Add 8 beans. Complete the first ten frame with 3 beans. Then, place 5 beans on the second ten frame. Fill in the recording sheet as shown below.

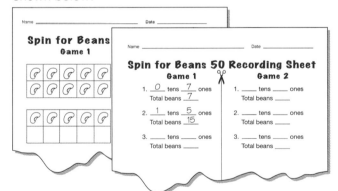

Figure 3: *Play for two spins of* Spin for Beans 50

TIMS Tip

Add *Spin for Beans 50* to the Games Menu.

As children play the game, ask questions such as the following:

- *Which player has more beans? How do you know?*
- *You have 34 beans. How many more do you need to get to 40 beans?*
- *You have 42 beans. Do you need more or less than 10 beans to get to 50 beans?*

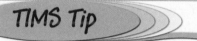

TIMS Tip

If students have trouble keeping the beans in their correct spot on the mat, have students place the beans, then take them off one by one and mark an "x" in each box.

Homework and Practice

- Students may demonstrate *Spin for Beans 50* to their parents and play at home. You may provide a resealable bag filled with beans for each student. Otherwise, parents may use pennies or other counters in place of beans. To play at home students will need their *Spin for Beans 50 Playing Mat,* the *Spin for Beans 50 Recording Sheet,* the *Spin for Beans 50* Game Page, and the *Spin for Beans at Home* Homework Page.

- DPP item E provides practice counting by tens and ones using a link chain.

Assessment

- As you observe children playing the game, assess the following skills:
  1. counting by tens and ones;
  2. naming using grouping language (e.g., 2 tens and 4 ones); and
  3. using conventional number names (e.g., 24).

- Use DPP item F to assess students' abilities to group and count pennies by tens and ones.

- Use the *Observational Assessment Record* to document students' abilities to group and count objects by tens and ones and to represent two-digit numbers using ten frames.

Name _____ Date _____

Spin for Beans at Home

📖Homework

Dear Family Member:

Your child has played the game *Spin for Beans 50* in school and is ready to teach it to someone at home. You may use coins, paper clips, several scraps of paper, or other small counters instead of beans. Help your child keep a record of the number of minutes he or she plays and the number of people he or she teaches to play the game. Use the enclosed copy of the *Spin for Beans 50* game board and game directions.

Thank you for your help.

Make a tally mark for each person you teach to play the game.

Tallies _____

Make a tally mark for every five minutes you play the game.

Tallies _____ Total Minutes _____

Parent's Signature _____

Child's Signature _____

Return this sheet to school by _____.

164   SG • Grade 1 • Unit 9 • Lesson 3   Spin for Beans

Student Guide - page 164

Estimated Class Sessions

1

At a Glance

Math Facts Strategies and Daily Practice and Problems

DPP item E practices grouping and counting with tens and ones.

Teaching the Game   (A7)

1. Review the directions for *Spin for Beans 50* on the *Spin for Beans 50* Game Page.
2. Play *Spin for Beans 50* with a volunteer using a transparency of the *Spin for Beans 50 Playing Mat*. Demonstrate how to record the number of beans on the *Spin for Beans 50 Recording Sheet*.
3. As children play the game, circulate and ask questions about the number of beans a player has and how many more he or she needs to win.

Homework

Students play *Spin for Beans 50* with a family member at home.

Assessment

1. As you observe children playing the game, assess the following skills:
   - counting by tens and ones;
   - naming using grouping language (e.g., 2 tens and 4 ones);
   - using conventional number names (e.g., 24).

   Use Assessment Indicator A1 and the *Observational Assessment Record* to record students' abilities with these skills.
2. Use DPP item F as an assessment.

Notes:

Spin for Beans 50 Recording Sheet

Game 1   ✂   Game 2

1. _____ tens _____ ones
Total beans _____

2. _____ tens _____ ones
Total beans _____

3. _____ tens _____ ones
Total beans _____

4. _____ tens _____ ones
Total beans _____

5. _____ tens _____ ones
Total beans _____

6. _____ tens _____ ones
Total beans _____

7. _____ tens _____ ones
Total beans _____

8. _____ tens _____ ones
Total beans _____

9. _____ tens _____ ones
Total beans _____

10. _____ tens _____ ones
Total beans _____

1. _____ tens _____ ones
Total beans _____

2. _____ tens _____ ones
Total beans _____

3. _____ tens _____ ones
Total beans _____

4. _____ tens _____ ones
Total beans _____

5. _____ tens _____ ones
Total beans _____

6. _____ tens _____ ones
Total beans _____

7. _____ tens _____ ones
Total beans _____

8. _____ tens _____ ones
Total beans _____

9. _____ tens _____ ones
Total beans _____

10. _____ tens _____ ones
Total beans _____

Name _____   Date _____

Spin for Beans 50 Playing Mat

Game 1   Game 2

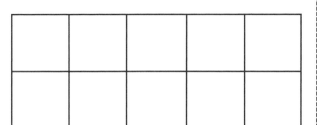
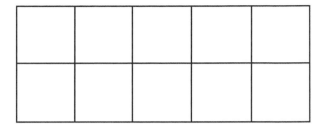

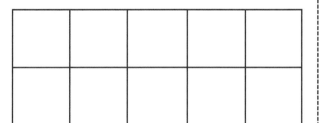
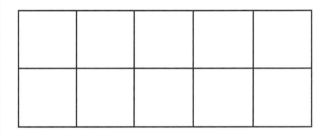

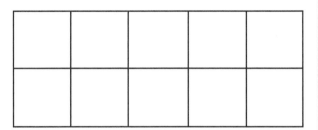
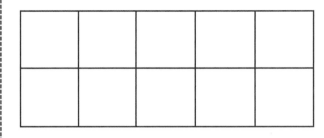

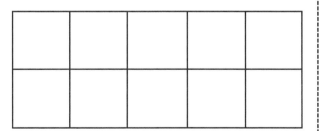
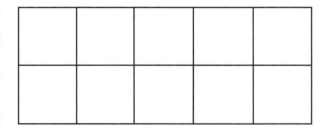

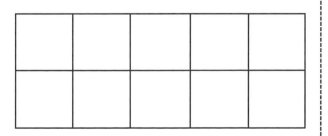
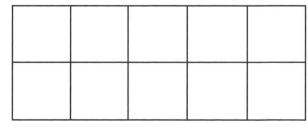

Lesson 4

The *50 Chart*

Lesson Overview

Estimated Class Sessions

1

In this activity, student pairs construct models by sorting different numbers of connecting cubes into groups of tens and ones. They lay each model on a *50 Chart* and then record its number of cubes on the chart. The goal is to illustrate the relationship between groupings of tens and ones and the sequence of two-digit numbers that is represented on the chart. After locating and recording selected numbers on the chart, students identify number patterns to complete the chart and discuss some of the number relationships represented.

Key Content

- Representing quantities to 50 using connecting cubes and a *50 Chart*.
- Representing two-digit numbers using grouping language (e.g., 6 tens and 3 ones) and conventional names (e.g., 63).
- Using number patterns to solve problems on the *50 Chart*.
- Communicating mathematics verbally and in writing.

Math Facts Strategies

DPP items G and H provide practice with addition and subtraction facts strategies.

Assessment

Use Assessment Indicator A3 and the *Observational Assessment Record* to record students' abilities to describe a number in relation to other numbers.

Curriculum Sequence

Before This Unit

Patterns on the *50 Chart* and the *100 Chart*

In Unit 5 Lesson 1, students briefly explored patterns created while skip counting on a *100 Chart*.

After This Unit

Patterns on the *50 Chart* and the *100 Chart*

Students use the *100 Chart* to investigate number patterns throughout first grade. For example, Unit 11 Lesson 4 uses the *100 Chart* in a game format. In Grade 2, students further explore number patterns using the *200 Chart*. See Grade 2 Unit 2 Lesson 2.

Materials List

Supplies and Copies

Student	Teacher
Supplies for Each Student Pair	**Supplies**
• 50 connecting cubes	• 50 overhead color tiles to represent connecting cubes, optional
	• index card with the number 32
Copies	**Copies/Transparencies**
• 1 copy of *Find the Numbers* per student pair (*Unit Resource Guide* Page 55)	• 1 transparency of *50 Chart* (*Student Guide* Page 165)

All blackline masters including assessment, transparency, and DPP masters are also on the Teacher Resource CD.

Student Books
50 Chart (*Student Guide* Page 165)

Daily Practice and Problems
DPP items G–H (*Unit Resource Guide* Page 16)

Assessment Tools
Observational Assessment Record (*Unit Resource Guide* Pages 11–12)

Suggestions for using the DPPs are on page 53.

G. Subtraction Facts 2 (URG p. 16)

  A. $8 - 6 =$

  B. $9 - 4 =$

  C. $32 - 3 =$

H. At the Circus (URG p. 16)

1. Todd counted 3 acrobats riding unicycles. Six acrobats were swinging on the trapeze. How many acrobats were performing at once?

2. Gwen counted 4 elephants in the first ring at the circus. She counted 5 in the second ring. There were 3 in the third ring. How many elephants were there altogether?

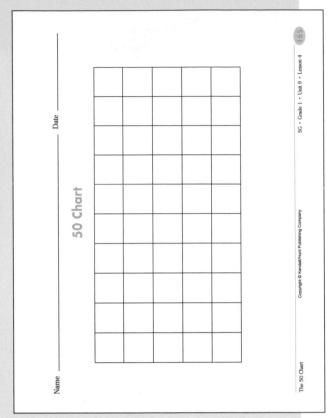

Student Guide - page 165 (Answers on p. 56)

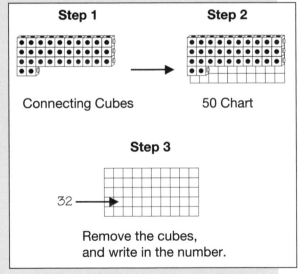

Figure 4: *Connecting cubes and* 50 *Chart*

Teaching the Activity

Part 1 **Representing Two-Digit Numbers with Connecting Cubes**

Review how to represent two-digit numbers with connecting cubes by selecting a number, such as today's date, and having students represent it with towers of tens and leftover ones.

Display the transparency of the *50 Chart* on the overhead. Hold up a card with "32" written on it, and explain that you are going to find this number on the *50 Chart* using connecting cubes. Using the cubes, collect three towers of ten cubes and two single cubes. Ask students to do the same. Beginning at the top of the chart, use the three towers of ten cubes each to cover three rows of ten squares and use the two individual cubes to cover two more squares in the fourth row. (See Figure 4.) Ask:

- *How many rows of ten squares and how many extra squares have I covered?* (3 and 2)

Remove the cubes and write "32" in the last square covered. Now, ask each pair to follow your example and cover their 50 charts with the cubes and record the number 32. Make sure students cover the chart beginning at the top left. Practice these same steps with a few other numbers that are not on the *Find the Numbers* Blackline Master.

Part 2 **Locating Numbers on the *50 Chart***

Using the method just described, have student pairs locate on the *50 Chart* the numbers on the *Find the Numbers* Blackline Master. You may fill in the four blank boxes at the bottom of the page as you choose, perhaps including different numbers for different student pairs. When students finish locating and recording the numbers, their charts should resemble Figure 5.

		3							
	12			15					20
21				25		28			
	32					37			40
		43		45				49	

Figure 5: *Partially completed* 50 *Chart*

Continue the activity by guiding students to fill in all the numbers on the chart. Ask:

- *What numbers belong in the first row?* (1–10)
- *What number belongs in the square immediately before 12?* (11)
- *What number belongs in the square just after 12?* (13)

Ask similar questions about other numbers that students have placed on the chart.

Encourage them to discuss the patterns they see and how those patterns can help them identify the missing numbers. Once students have filled in all the numbers in their charts, have pairs trade charts and check each other's work.

Conclude the activity by discussing the chart's structure and patterns. Name a number on the chart, and ask students to identify other related numbers. For example, ask:

- *What is the number in the row above 15?* (5)
- *How much more is 15 than the number in the row above it?* (10 more)
- *What number is directly below the number 37?* (47)
- *How much less is 37 than the number in the row below 37?* (10 less)

Invite students to think of other similar questions about the chart for the class to answer.

Math Facts Strategies

DPP item G practices subtraction facts strategies. Item H asks students to solve addition word problems.

Assessment

Use the *Observational Assessment Record* to document students' abilities to describe a number in relation to other numbers.

Math Facts Strategies and Daily Practice and Problems

DPP items G and H practice addition and subtraction facts strategies.

Part 1. Representing Two-Digit Numbers with Connecting Cubes (A2) (A7)

1. Students represent a two-digit number with connecting cube towers of tens and ones.
2. Model covering the *50 Chart* transparency with 32 cubes on the overhead projector.
3. Remove the connecting cubes and write "32" in the last square covered.
4. Students cover their charts with 32 cubes, beginning at the top left, and record the number 32 in the correct box. Try other examples.

Part 2. Locating Numbers on the *50 Chart* (A3)

1. Students fill in the *50 Chart* with numbers from the *Find the Numbers* Blackline Master.
2. Students then use connecting cubes to fill in all other squares on their chart and discuss patterns that emerge.
3. Students exchange papers to check each other's work.
4. Discuss the chart's structure and patterns.
5. Ask students to identify specific numbers on the chart given clues about their location.

Assessment

Use Assessment Indicator A3 and the *Observational Assessment Record* to record students' abilities to describe a number in relation to other numbers.

Answer Key is on page 56.

Notes:

Find the Numbers

12	25	37	21
15	40	45	20
28	43	3	49

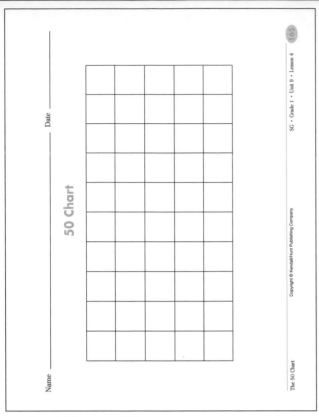

Student Guide - page 165

Student Guide (p. 165)

50 Chart

1	2	3	4	5	6	7	8	9	10
11	12	13	14	15	16	17	18	19	20
21	22	23	24	25	26	27	28	29	30
31	32	33	34	35	36	37	38	39	40
41	42	43	44	45	46	47	48	49	50

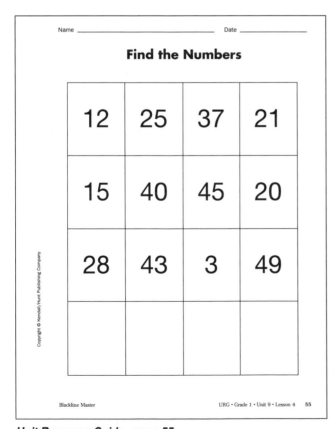

Unit Resource Guide - page 55

Unit Resource Guide (p. 55)

Find the Numbers

See Figure 5 in Lesson Guide 4.*

*Answers and/or discussion are included in the Lesson Guide.

Lesson 5

The *100 Chart*

Lesson Overview

Estimated Class Sessions

2

This activity focuses on number patterns and number relationships to reinforce students' familiarity with the counting sequence to 100. Students practice skip counting by twos, fives, and tens. They learn that 10 tens is 100. They identify number patterns to fill in the *100 Chart*. And, finally, they solve a number mystery using clues about number relationships.

Key Content

- Exploring relationships among numbers to 100.
- Exploring number patterns in skip counting on the *100 Chart*.
- Communicating mathematics verbally and in writing.
- Using number patterns to solve problems on the *100 Chart*.
- Representing numbers on the *100 Chart*.
- Counting by twos, fives, and tens.

Key Vocabulary

- between
- closer to
- halfway
- interval
- less than
- more than

Math Facts Strategies

Item L provides practice with subtraction facts strategies.

Homework

Students complete *Counting by Tens* Homework Page at home after completing the first column in class.

Assessment

1. Make additional copies of the *Target Numbers* Blackline Master and give students a new set of numbers to fill in the center boxes of the five-square segments. Ask them to fill in the blank boxes as before.
2. Use Assessment Indicators A2, A3, and A7 and the *Observational Assessment Record* to record students' abilities to count by twos, fives, and tens, to describe a number in relation to other numbers, and to represent two-digit numbers using *100 Charts*.

Materials List

Supplies and Copies

Student	Teacher
Supplies for Each Student Pair • 100 connecting cubes grouped in tens	**Supplies** • overhead color tiles to represent connecting cubes, optional
Copies • 2 copies of *Target Numbers* per student (*Unit Resource Guide* Page 65) • 1 copy of *Tricky Target Numbers* per student, optional (*Unit Resource Guide* Page 66) • 1 copy of *Desk-Size 100 Chart* per student, optional (*Unit Resource Guide* Page 67)	**Copies/Transparencies** • 1 transparency of *100 Chart* (*Student Guide* Page 167)

All blackline masters including assessment, transparency, and DPP masters are also on the Teacher Resource CD.

Student Books

100 Chart (*Student Guide* Page 167)
Counting by Tens (*Student Guide* Page 169)

Daily Practice and Problems

DPP items I–L (*Unit Resource Guide* Pages 17–19)

Assessment Tools

Observational Assessment Record (*Unit Resource Guide* Pages 11–12)

Daily Practice and Problems

Suggestions for using the DPPs are on page 63.

I. Number of Letters (URG p. 17)

Joseph made this table for the names of his family members.

First Name	Number of Letters
Joseph	6
May	3
Elizabeth	9
Charlie	7

1. What is the total number of letters Joseph recorded for his family?
2. Which name has the most letters?
3. Which name has the least letters?
4. How many more letters are in the longest name than in the shortest name?

J. Patterns (URG p. 18)

Write A, B, or C under each object to show the pattern. Circle the repeating pattern unit.

1. △ △ ○ △ △ ○ △ △ ○

2. ▯ ▯ ▢ ▢ ○ ○ ▯ ▯ ▢

K. Names and Letters (URG p. 18)

In Miss White's class, five students reported the total number of letters in the names they collected.

Sally's family: 32 letters
Roberto's gerbil family: 12 letters
Mary's family: 28 letters
Sam's family: 15 letters
Joseph's family: 25 letters

1. Predict whether these five students will have more or less than 100 letters total.
2. Use a calculator to check your prediction. List the keys you pressed on the calculator to get your answer.

L. Subtraction Facts 3 (URG p. 19)

A. $6 - 3 =$

B. $11 - 5 =$

C. $27 - 4 =$

Name _____ **Date** _____

100 Chart

1	2	3	4	5	6	7	8	9	10
11	12	13	14	15	16	17	18	19	20
21	22	23	24	25	26	27	28	29	30
31	32	33	34	35	36	37	38	39	40
41	42	43	44	45	46	47	48	49	50
51	52	53	54	55	56	57	58	59	60
61	62	63	64	65	66	67	68	69	70
71	72	73	74	75	76	77	78	79	80
81	82	83	84	85	86	87	88	89	90
91	92	93	94	95	96	97	98	99	100

The 100 Chart   SG • Grade 1 • Unit 9 • Lesson 5   **167**

Student Guide - page 167

Teaching the Activity

Display the transparency of the *100 Chart* Activity Page on the overhead projector. Explain that the chart is the same as the *50 Chart* except the numbers go up to 100. Remind students that they used the *100 Chart* to record skip counting in Unit 5. Ask them to locate numbers from clues you give them like the ones listed below. Encourage them to explain how they determine their answers.

- *I'm thinking of the number that is 2 tens and 5 ones.* (25)
- *I'm thinking of the number that is one more than 32.* (33)
- *I'm thinking of the number that is two less than 70.* (68)
- *I'm thinking of the number that is ten more than 90.* (100)

Part 1 **Skip Counting by Twos, Fives, and Tens**

Have students begin working on the *100 Chart* Activity Page by asking them to count out loud by twos to 40. Help them get started by naming the first several numbers in the sequence: 2, 4, 6, 8. . . . Have students repeat the count by twos to 40, placing a cube on each number on the chart as they say it. When they have finished counting and placing cubes, ask:

- *Do you see any patterns on the chart?*

For example, since students were introduced to even and odd numbers prior to this lesson (Unit 4 Lesson 1), some may recognize skip counting by twos as reciting even numbers.

- *Will we cover the number 52 if we continued counting?* (Yes.) *How about 76? 85?*

Encourage them to explain their reasoning. Remove the cubes from the chart and repeat the same procedure, this time counting by fives to 50. Ask questions such as:

- *What patterns do you see now?* (Students may recognize that the numbers we say form the middle and last columns in the *100 Chart.* Also, the numbers all end in a 5 or 0.)
- *Will we cover 85 if we continue counting?* (Yes.)
- *Will we cover 76 if we continue counting?* (No.)

Once students are comfortable counting by twos and fives, review counting by tens. Students may remember using their hands and counting their fingers in groups of five and ten in Unit 5 Lesson 2. Have student pairs show ten stacks of ten cubes on their desks and count them by tens to 100. Emphasize that 10 tens is the same as 100. Have students count by tens to 100 again, this time placing a cube on each number on the chart as it is said, i.e., 10, 20, 30. . . . Encourage them to describe any patterns they see on the chart.

Ask each student pair to put four cubes in front of them. Then, have them add one stack of ten cubes to the four cubes and identify the total number of cubes. Have them add another stack of ten cubes and identify the new number of cubes. Repeat this process until they reach 94. Ask students to count by ten starting at the number 4 again, this time placing a single cube on each number on the chart as it is said: 4, 14, 24 . . . . Encourage them to discuss patterns they see. Help students recognize that each number has 4 ones and is ten more than the last (the second digit or the ones digit in each number is the same—4). Record the numbers in a column on the board as children say them aloud. Repeat this with several other starting numbers.

Part 2 Targeting Numbers on the *100 Chart*

Display a transparency of the *100 Chart* on the overhead projector, and circle the target number 25 on the chart. Ask children to identify the following numbers and circle them on the chart as you go:

- one less than 25 (24)
- one more than 25 (26)
- ten less than 25 (15)
- ten more than 25 (35)

Repeat this exercise using other numbers such as 12 and 38. Ask students to explain their reasoning; then, have them verify their answers using cubes stacked in groups of tens and ones.

Ask:

- *What do you notice happening when we move to the left on the chart?* (Numbers get smaller. We are taking away or subtracting.)
- *What do you notice when we move to the right?* (Numbers get larger. We are adding.)
- *What do you notice when we move up one row?* (Numbers get smaller. We subtract. The second digit is the same.)
- *What do you notice when we move down one row?* (Numbers get larger. We add. The second digit is the same.)

Write a number in each center box of the *Target Numbers* Activity Page before copying it for students. Explain that each five-square segment shows part of the *100 Chart*, and their job is to fill in the missing numbers for each segment. Invite them to share their results and discuss any patterns they discover. For example, students may say:

- The numbers above and below one another differ by ten.

- Numbers to the right and left of each other differ by one.

- Numbers above and below each other end in the same number (the ones digit is the same).

- Numbers to the right and left of each other start with the same number (the tens digit is the same).

Part 3 **Exploring Relationships with Numbers to 100**

This final part of the lesson gives students more opportunity to explore number relationships such as **between, interval, closer to, halfway between, more than,** and **less than.** To develop these concepts, use problems such as the one listed below. Always encourage students to explain their reasoning when discussing solutions.

1. Tell students you want them to solve a number mystery using clues you give them. Begin by saying, *"I'm thinking of a number that is between 30 and 40."* Put your fingers on the numbers 30 and 40 on the *100 Chart* transparency to show students the interval. Say, *"These numbers are **between** 30 and 40. The number I'm thinking of is in this **interval**."* Ask them to point to the possible numbers on their *100 Charts*.

2. Say, *"The number is **closer to** 40 than to 30."* Ask them to show which numbers on the chart this could be.

3. Finally, tell them, *"The number is two **more than** 35."* Have them identify the number and discuss the reasoning they used to solve the mystery.

DPP item L provides practice with subtraction facts strategies.

Homework and Practice

- Have students look at the *Counting by Tens* Homework Page. Explain that they are to count by tens to determine the missing numbers in each column. The first column is partially complete to help students see the pattern. Complete the first one in class to make sure students understand the assignment. Have them take home the *100 Chart* for help filling in each column on the Homework Page and coloring each corresponding column on the *100 Chart*.

- DPP item I practices reading and interpreting data in a table. Item J examines AAB and AABBCC patterns. Item K reviews reading and interpreting data and making predictions.

Assessment

- Make additional copies of the *Target Numbers* Activity Page and give students a new set of numbers to fill in the center boxes of the five-square segments. Ask them to fill in the blank boxes as before.

- Use the *Observational Assessment Record* to document students' abilities to count by twos, fives, and tens, to describe a number in relation to other numbers, and to represent two-digit numbers using *100 Charts*.

Extension

- Make copies of the *Tricky Target Numbers* Activity Page for students who are ready for more work with the *100 Chart*.

- Have each student cut out and tape the *Desk-Size 100 Chart* to his or her desk. Occasionally, invite students to look for patterns in the chart. Given the opportunity to explore independently, children will discover many patterns and relationships in the chart. For example, some will find ways of adding and subtracting two-digit numbers.

Name _____ Date _____

Counting by Tens

Homework

Count by tens. Fill in the missing numbers. Then, color the *100 Chart*.

yellow	green	orange	blue	red	purple
8	10	2			
18					
28			25		
38					36
				51	

The 100 Chart   SG • Grade 1 • Unit 9 • Lesson 5   169

Student Guide - page 169 (Answers on p. 68)

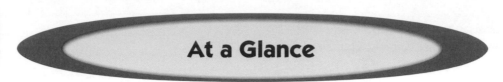
Math Facts Strategies and Daily Practice and Problems

DPP items I and K use data to solve problems. Item J reviews patterns. Item L practices subtraction facts strategies.

Part 1. Skip Counting by Twos, Fives, and Tens   (A2) (A7)

1. Give students clues to locate numbers on the *100 Chart* transparency.
2. Skip count by twos to 40, and place a cube on each number said aloud. Discuss patterns.
3. Skip count by fives and place a cube on each number said aloud. Discuss patterns.
4. Skip count by tens to 100 and place a cube on each number said. Discuss patterns.
5. Students keep adding stacks of ten cubes to a stack of four cubes until they reach 94.
6. Students, starting at four, skip count by tens and place cubes on each number said.

Part 2. Targeting Numbers on the *100 Chart*   (A3) (A7)

1. Students identify and circle numbers to the right and left of given numbers and above and below given numbers.
2. Students complete the *Target Numbers* Blackline Master.

Part 3. Exploring Relationships with Numbers to 100   (A3) (A7)

Give students clues to mystery numbers on the chart by using the concepts between, interval, closer to, halfway between, more than, and less than.

Homework

Students complete *Counting by Tens* Homework Page at home after completing the first column in class.

Assessment

1. Make additional copies of the *Target Numbers* Blackline Master and give students a new set of numbers to fill in the center boxes of the five-square segments. Ask them to fill in the blank boxes as before.
2. Use Assessment Indicators A2, A3, and A7 and the *Observational Assessment Record* to record students' abilities to count by twos, fives, and tens, to describe a number in relation to other numbers, and to represent two-digit numbers using *100 Charts*.

Extension

1. Use the *Tricky Target Numbers* Activity Page with students who are ready for more *100 Chart* work.
2. Have students look for patterns in their *Desk-Size 100 Charts*.

Answer Key is on pages 68–69.

Notes:

Target Numbers

Your teacher wrote a number in each center box. Fill in the remaining blank boxes with a number from the *100 Chart.*

What patterns do you see?

Tricky Target Numbers

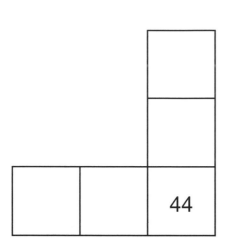

44

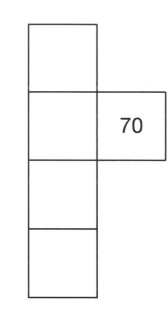

70

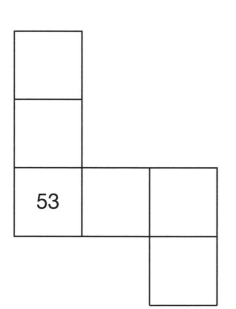

53

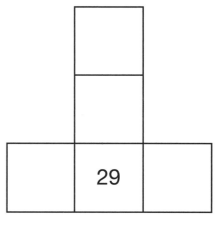

29

Write your own number in the box with the circle.
Then, fill in the other boxes.

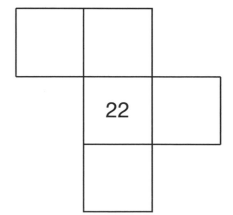

22

Desk-Size 100 Chart

100 Chart									
1	2	3	4	5	6	7	8	9	10
11	12	13	14	15	16	17	18	19	20
21	22	23	24	25	26	27	28	29	30
31	32	33	34	35	36	37	38	39	40
41	42	43	44	45	46	47	48	49	50
51	52	53	54	55	56	57	58	59	60
61	62	63	64	65	66	67	68	69	70
71	72	73	74	75	76	77	78	79	80
81	82	83	84	85	86	87	88	89	90
91	92	93	94	95	96	97	98	99	100

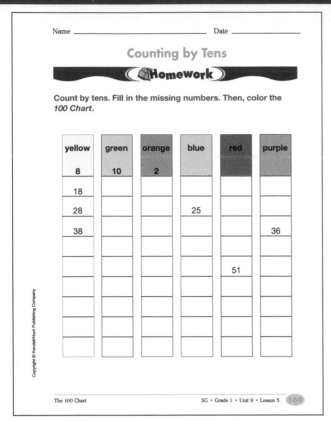

Student Guide - page 169

Student Guide (p. 169)

Counting by Tens*

yellow: 8, 18, 28, 38, 48, 58, 68, 78, 88, 98

green: 10, 20, 30, 40, 50, 60, 70, 80, 90, 100

orange: 2, 12, 22, 32, 42, 52, 62, 72, 82, 92

blue: 5, 15, 25, 35, 45, 55, 65, 75, 85, 95

red: 1, 11, 21, 31, 41, 51, 61, 71, 81, 91

purple: 6, 16, 26, 36, 46, 56, 66, 76, 86, 96

Unit Resource Guide - page 65

Unit Resource Guide (p. 65)

Target Numbers

Answers will vary depending upon numbers filled in.*

*Answers and/or discussion are included in the Lesson Guide.

Unit Resource Guide (p. 66)

Tricky Target Numbers

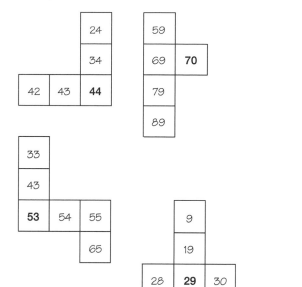

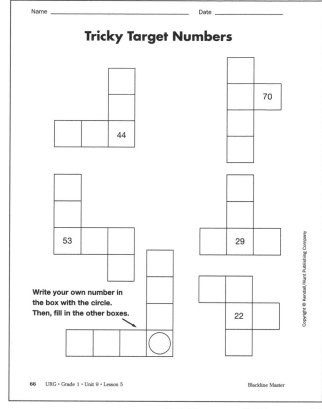

Unit Resource Guide - page 66

Lesson 6

Measuring with Connecting Links

Estimated Class Sessions

1

Lesson Overview

In this activity, students continue to explore two-digit numbers. They place numbers into intervals and identify numbers that are "close to" given numbers. Students measure objects using links, record the lengths in tens and ones, and place them into intervals of 20. Students develop number sense as they visually check the placement of the links in intervals.

Key Content

- Measuring length using nonstandard units (links).
- Investigating number relationships: placing numbers into intervals.
- Representing numbers with connecting links.
- Comparing and ordering two-digit numbers.
- Communicating mathematics verbally and in writing.

Homework

Students play *Guess My Number* at home.

Assessment

Use Assessment Indicator A4 and the *Observational Assessment Record* to record students' abilities to measure length in nonstandard units.

Curriculum Sequence

Before This Unit

Number Relationships

In kindergarten and in Grade 1 Units 1–8, students described number relationships through the language of comparison. For example, in Unit 1 students compared numbers using more, less, and about the same. In Unit 6 Lesson 2 *Rolling Along with Links,* students compared lengths and placed numbers into intervals.

After This Unit

Number Relationships

Students continue to compare numbers and place them into intervals. For example, in Unit 10 Lessons 2 and 3, students compare areas of shapes. In Unit 11 Lesson 5 *How Long Is 100?* students place numbers into intervals. In the laboratory investigation in Unit 11 Lesson 6 *Weather 2: Winter Skies,* students compare their data using bar graphs.

Materials List

Supplies and Copies

Student	Teacher
Supplies for Each Student Pair • 2 index cards • 100 connecting links in different colored ten-link chains • masking tape	**Supplies** • easel paper, optional • 15 index cards for the Extension
Copies • 1 copy of *Desk-Size 100 Chart* per student (*Unit Resource Guide* Page 67) • 1 copy of *100 Chart* per student, optional (*Unit Resource Guide* Page 76)	**Copies/Transparencies**

All blackline masters including assessment, transparency, and DPP masters are also on the Teacher Resource CD.

Student Books
Guess My Number (*Student Guide* Page 171)

Daily Practice and Problems
DPP items M–N (*Unit Resource Guide* Pages 19–20)

Assessment Tools
Observational Assessment Record (*Unit Resource Guide* Pages 11–12)

Daily Practice and Problems

Suggestions for using the DPPs are on page 74.

M. 100 Chart (URG p. 19)   Ⓝ

1. What number is above 14 on the *100 Chart?*
2. What number is below 14 on the *100 Chart?*
3. What number is to the right of 14? to the left?
4. I am on 14. I move 3 spaces to the right. What number do I land on?
5. I am on 14. I move 3 spaces to the left. What number do I land on?

N. I'm Thinking of a Number   Ⓝ
   (URG p. 20)

What number am I thinking of?

1. I am thinking of a number that is 2 tens and 3 ones.
2. I am thinking of a number that is 2 more than 17.
3. I am thinking of a number that is 4 more than 28.
4. I am thinking of a number that is 3 less than 75.
5. I am thinking of a number that is 6 less than 43.
6. I am thinking of a number that is 10 more than 67.

Before the Activity

Draw four sections of number intervals, as shown in Figure 6, on the board or easel paper.

Figure 6: *Intervals of 20*

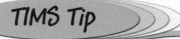
Teaching the Activity

Instruct each pair of students to make an 80-link chain that alternates colors in groups of ten links. Have pairs check one another's chains by holding them next to each other to see that the ten-link sections match. Give each pair two index cards and have them follow these steps:

1. Select two objects to measure whose lengths range between one link and 80 links (e.g., doors, books, desks, pencils).

2. Measure each object with the chain, breaking the chain to show the object's length.

3. Draw the object on an index card, and write its length (in links) next to it.

4. Tape the cards and the link chain in the appropriate interval on the board or easel paper. (See Figure 7.)

As students finish taping up their cards and chains, invite them to discuss their measuring results. Ask them to explain how they chose intervals. Choose one of the chains (e.g., a 32-link chain) and ask:

• *Why should 32 be placed in the 21–40 interval?*

Point out that the chain belongs in this interval because it has 3 tens and 2 ones, which is between 2 tens and 4 tens. You may need to hold up a chain that is 20 links long and a chain that is 40 links long for some students to see that a chain of 32 links goes between these two chains. Repeat this questioning process for other numbers. Then have students verify that their chain is in the correct interval by comparing their chain to adjacent chains.

Choose cards that have been posted for two different objects, such as the board tray (e.g., 56 links long) and the door (e.g., 68 links long). Ask:

• *Which number is greater? Can you tell which is longer by looking at the tray and the door?*

After letting them make predictions, have them verify their answers by comparing, in this case, a 56-link chain and a 68-link chain.

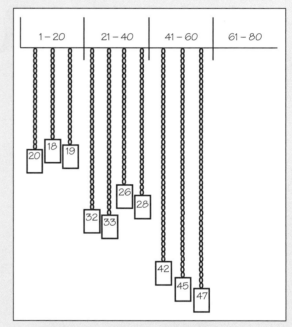

Figure 7: *Placing chains in intervals*

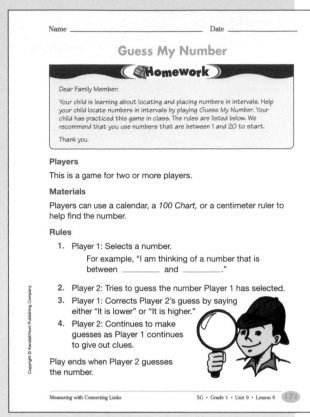

Student Guide - page 171

Use clues such as the following to help reinforce number relationship concepts. After each clue, ask students to show the number(s) on their *100 Charts*.

- My number is between 60 and 80.
- My number is closer to 60.
- My number is halfway between 60 and 70.

Students should be able to verify these locations with their link chains.

Homework and Practice

- Encourage students to play "Guess My Number" at home. The *Guess My Number* Homework Page provides simple directions. Play this game a few times in class to familiarize students. A sample game is provided here.

  Select a number and keep it secret. The child tries to guess it with intervals and clues. For example,

  Player 1: Thinks of a number. "I am thinking of a number that is between 0 and 20."

  Player 2: "Is it 10?"

  Player 1: "No, it is lower."

  Player 2: "Is it higher or lower than 5?"

  Player 1: "Higher."

  Player 2: "So it is between 5 and 10. Is it 7?"

  Player 1: "No, it's lower." Etc.

  Students can use a calendar, centimeter ruler, or a *100 Chart* to narrow down their guesses.

- For DPP item M, students practice describing numbers in relation to other numbers using the *100 Chart.* Item N asks students to name numbers given in groups of tens and ones.

Assessment

Use the *Observational Assessment Record* to document students' abilities to measure length in nonstandard units.

Extension

Write numbers between 20 and 80 on index cards. Give two or three cards to each student pair. Have them determine in which interval each number should go and tell which number is the greatest and which is the least. Have students explain their answers and check them with link chains.

At a Glance

Math Facts Strategies and Daily Practice and Problems

DPP items M and N build number sense.

Teaching the Activity

1. Draw four sections of number intervals on chart paper or the board.
2. Students make an 80-link chain of alternating ten-link colors.
3. Students select objects to measure, draw the object and record its length on an index card, and tape the card and the chain in the appropriate interval on the board.
4. Students discuss their measurements and the intervals shown.
5. Students compare lengths in intervals and verify their solutions by comparing link chains.

Homework

Students play *Guess My Number* at home.

Assessment

Use Assessment Indicator A4 and the *Observational Assessment Record* to record students' abilities to measure length in nonstandard units.

Extension

Write numbers between 20 and 80 on index cards and have students place the numbers in intervals and tell which number is the least or greatest.

Notes:

100 Chart

1	2	3	4	5	6	7	8	9	10
11	12	13	14	15	16	17	18	19	20
21	22	23	24	25	26	27	28	29	30
31	32	33	34	35	36	37	38	39	40
41	42	43	44	45	46	47	48	49	50
51	52	53	54	55	56	57	58	59	60
61	62	63	64	65	66	67	68	69	70
71	72	73	74	75	76	77	78	79	80
81	82	83	84	85	86	87	88	89	90
91	92	93	94	95	96	97	98	99	100

Lesson 7

Numbers in the News

Lesson Overview

Estimated Class Sessions

1

This activity explores the relative size among numbers. Using two-digit numbers in newspaper headlines, children describe the relationship of one number to others.

Key Content

- Developing number sense for two-digit numbers.
- Describing numbers in relation to other numbers.
- Communicating mathematics verbally and in writing.
- Connecting mathematics to real-world situations: numbers in newspapers.
- Comparing two-digit numbers using more, less, about the same, between, and close.

Homework

Assign the *Find Numbers in the News* Homework Pages.

Assessment

1. Use the Journal Prompt as an assessment.
2. Use Assessment Indicator A3 and the *Observational Assessment Record* to record students' abilities to describe a number in relation to other numbers.

Materials List

Supplies and Copies

Student	Teacher
Supplies for Each Student Pair • newspaper headline • piece of easel paper • old newspapers, optional • 100 connecting cubes, optional	**Supplies** • easel paper • scissors
Copies • 1 copy of *Desk-Size 100 Chart* per student, optional (*Unit Resource Guide* Page 67) • 1 headline from *Numbers in the News* per student pair, optional (*Unit Resource Guide* Page 83)	**Copies/Transparencies**

All blackline masters including assessment, transparency, and DPP masters are also on the Teacher Resource CD.

Student Books
100 Chart (*Student Guide* Page 167), optional
Find Numbers in the News (*Student Guide* Pages 173–174)

Daily Practice and Problems
DPP items O–P (*Unit Resource Guide* Page 21)

Assessment Tools
Observational Assessment Record (*Unit Resource Guide* Pages 11–12)

Daily Practice and Problems

Suggestions for using the DPPs are on page 81.

O. Skip Counting on the Calculator
(URG p. 21)

1. Press 1 + 5 = on your calculator.
2. Circle the answer on the *100 Chart*.
3. Continue to press the equal sign and circle each result on the chart until no more numbers can be circled.
4. Describe the patterns you see.

P. Spin for Beans 50 (URG p. 21)

1. Marissa and Tyrone are playing *Spin for Beans 50.* Marissa has 4 full ten frames and 6 leftovers. Tyrone has 3 full frames and 9 leftovers. Who is winning?
2. How many more beans does Marissa need to reach 50?
3. How many more beans does Tyrone need to reach 50?

Give each student pair old newspapers to find a newspaper headline that contains a two-digit number. Or, if
you prefer, cut out the headlines from the *Numbers in
the News* Blackline Master, and distribute one headline to each pair. Each pair will need a large sheet of
easel paper. You will need one as well. Paste each
headline at the top of a piece of easel paper.

Write the headline shown in Figure 8, "34 Kids
Think in Math Marathon," at the top of a piece
of easel paper. Read it to the class and begin a
discussion about the number 34 by asking the
following questions:

* *Do you think this is a large number?*

* *Do you think this is a small number?*

* *How does it compare to the number of children in
  our class?*

* *What numbers is it close to?*

As you and the children discuss these questions,
encourage them to make comparative statements
about the number 34. (See Figure 8 for examples.)
Record students' statements under the headline.
Invite them to write their own comparative statements under the headline.

Have each student pair write interesting statements
about the number in their own headline. Ask them to
write at least six things, explaining that they can look
at the posted class statements to get ideas. Encourage
students to use the *100 Chart* to help them.

When students are finished, have each pair look over
their work to see if they believe they have written
correct statements about their number. Post these
pages around the classroom for everyone to study.
Select some statements to discuss with the class,
asking students to find a way to verify that they are
correct. They can use *100 Charts* or connecting
cubes. Help students change incorrect statements
without singling out individuals who have made mis-
takes. Encourage children to add new statements to
each other's papers.

TIMS Tip

Children may describe 34 in terms of partitions (e.g., 34 is
20 + 10 + 4), as they have done in previous units. However, the
focus in this activity should be on the relationship of a given
number to other numbers.

---

34 Kids Think in Math Marathon

34 is
* large compared to 5;
* about the same size as 30;
* a lot less than 100;
* between 30 and 40;
* 10 more than 24;
* 10 less than 44;
* 1 more than 33;
* 1 less than 35.

Figure 8: *News headline and
number statements*

Journal Prompt

My (mom, dad, grandmother, grandfather, uncle, aunt) is _____
years old. (Students can make a good guess.) Four things I know
about the number are . . .

- Assign the *Find Numbers in the News* Homework Pages. Family members are asked to help children find a newspaper headline that contains a number. Then, students write sentences that compare their numbers to other numbers. Sample headlines and sentences are provided.

- DPP item O practices skip counting on the calculator. Item P reviews the game *Spin for Beans 50.*

Assessment

Assess students' knowledge of number relationships by reviewing the statements they wrote in response to the Journal Prompt. Use the *Observational Assessment Record* to document students' abilities to describe a number in relation to other numbers.

Name _____ Date _____

Find Numbers in the News

Homework

Dear Family Member:

Help your child find a newspaper headline with a number in it. Glue the headline in the space provided on the back of this paper. If your child cannot find one in the newspaper, circle one of the headlines below.

To get your child started, write one sentence that compares the number to other numbers. For example, 34 is 10 more than 24. More examples are listed for the number 34 below.

Encourage your child to think of his or her own sentences. He or she should record them on the lines provided on the back of this paper.

Thank you for your cooperation.

13-Hour Sale

32 TOTAL BODY EXERCISES

Dist. 87 gets tougher on bad checks

34 Kids Think in Math Marathon

34 is
- large compared to 5;
- about the same size as 30;
- a lot less than 100;
- between 30 and 40;
- 10 more than 24;
- 10 less than 44;
- 1 more than 33;
- 1 less than 35.

60 years later, medals honor veterans of World War II

Numbers in the News   SG • Grade 1 • Unit 9 • Lesson 7   173

Student Guide - page 173 (Answers on p. 84)

Name _____ Date _____

Paste your headline below.

174   SG • Grade 1 • Unit 9 • Lesson 7   Numbers in the News

Student Guide - page 174 (Answers on p. 84)

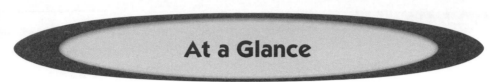

At a Glance

Math Facts Strategies and Daily Practice and Problems

DPP items O and P develop number sense for two-digit numbers.

Teaching the Activity (A3)

1. Each student pair finds one newspaper headline that contains a two-digit number.
2. Write the headline "34 Kids Think in Math Marathon" at the top of a piece of easel paper.
3. Read the headline to the class and discuss the number 34.
4. Encourage students to make comparative statements about the number 34.
5. Record students' statements under the headline on the easel paper.
6. On easel paper, each pair writes at least six interesting statements about the number in their headline.
7. Each pair looks over their work to check the accuracy of statements about their number.
8. Post these pages around the classroom for everyone to study and discuss.
9. Encourage students to add new statements to each other's papers.

Homework

Assign the *Find Numbers in the News* Homework Pages.

Assessment

1. Use the Journal Prompt as an assessment.
2. Use Assessment Indicator A3 and the *Observational Assessment Record* to record students' abilities to describe a number in relation to other numbers.

Answer Key is on page 84.

Notes:

Numbers in the News

Club ponders 80-year-old ban

13-Hour Sale

**BIGGEST SALE
EVER FOR OUR
60TH YEAR!**

20 years later,
'Welcome home'

Dist. 87 gets
tougher on
bad checks

60 years later, medals honor
veterans of World War II

25 Years and Ticking

**A plea for Puerto Rico:
Make us the 51st state**

30-DAY IN-HOME TRIAL!

18-HOUR SALE

Student Guide - page 173

Student Guide - page 174

Student Guide (pp. 173–174)

Find Numbers in the News

Answers will vary.

Lesson 8

Full of Beans

Lesson Overview

This lab helps students build ideas about volume and relative sizes of units. It also provides a context for students to apply the mathematical ideas they learned in this unit.

First, student groups fill a 2-ounce cup to the rim with small beans (e.g., kidney beans) and another cup with larger beans (e.g., large lima beans). They then count the beans in each cup by putting them into sections of a modified egg carton, ten beans in each section. The groups pool their data and graph the middle, or median, number.

Key Content

- Grouping and counting objects by tens and ones.
- Exploring volume measurement (capacity).
- Making and interpreting bar graphs.
- Exploring the inverse relationship between the unit's size and the number of units needed to measure a container's volume.
- Checking the reasonableness of measurements by comparing data.
- Using data to solve problems involving volume.
- Communicating mathematics verbally and in writing.

Key Vocabulary

- capacity
- median
- volume

Assessment

1. Use the *Maria and José's Graph* Assessment Page.
2. Fill a small container with a group of objects and another identical container with a group of larger objects. Label one jar A and the other B. Ask students to estimate how many objects are in each container and record their estimates and reasoning in their journals.
3. Use DPP item S as a short assessment.
4. Use Assessment Indicators A5 and A6 and the *Observational Assessment Record* to document students' abilities to make and interpret bar graphs and to use data to solve problems involving volume.
5. Transfer appropriate documentation from the Unit 9 *Observational Assessment Record* to students' *Individual Assessment Record Sheets*.

Curriculum Sequence

The TIMS Laboratory Method

Students used the TIMS Laboratory Method in Units 2, 5, and 6.

Volume

Students explored volume measurement in kindergarten in Month 8 Lessons 5 and 6.

The TIMS Laboratory Method

Students use the TIMS Laboratory Method in Units 11, 14, 16, and 19.

Volume

In Unit 12 students use connecting cubes to explore the volume of solid objects measured in cubic units. Students measure volume by displacement in Grade 2 Unit 10.

Materials List

Supplies and Copies

Student	Teacher
Supplies for Each Student Pair	**Supplies**
• 2 two-ounce cups • enough large beans (kidney) to fill a two-ounce cup, approximately 40 beans • enough small beans (large lima) to fill a two-ounce cup, approximately 80 beans • modified egg carton or 2 copies of *Ten Frames* (*Unit Resource Guide* Page 31)	• 2 large containers for the beans • 2 same-size jars: one filled with small objects and one filled with similar, but larger objects
Copies	**Copies/Transparencies**
• 2 copies of *Ten Frames* per student pair (*Unit Resource Guide* Page 31) or modified egg carton	• 1 transparency of *Full of Beans* (*Student Guide* Pages 175–178)

All blackline masters including assessment, transparency, and DPP masters are also on the Teacher Resource CD.

Student Books

Full of Beans (*Student Guide* Pages 175–178)
Maria and José's Graph (*Student Guide* Page 179)

Daily Practice and Problems

DPP items Q–V (*Unit Resource Guide* Pages 22–24)

Assessment Tools

Observational Assessment Record (*Unit Resource Guide* Pages 11–12)
Individual Assessment Record Sheet (*Teacher Implementation Guide,* Assessment section)

Daily Practice and Problems

Suggestions for using the DPPs are on page 90.

Q. Guess My Number (URG p. 22)

I am thinking of a number. Guess what it is. After each guess I will tell you whether you should guess higher or lower.

R. Skip Counting from Zero (URG p. 22)

1. If we skip count by twos, will we reach 47? 58?
2. If we skip count by fives, will we reach 45? 54?
3. If we skip count by tens, will we reach 100? 11?

S. Naming Numbers (URG p. 23)

1. Name a number between 40 and 50.
2. Name a number between 40 and 50 that is closer to 40 than 50.
3. Name a number halfway between 40 and 50.
4. Name a number more than 50.
5. Name a number less than 40.

T. Measuring with Links (URG p. 23)

Rita measured the width of a bookcase with her 80-link chain. She reported that the bookcase was 2 groups of ten links and 1 more link wide.

Nick measured the width of a window. He reported that the window was 19 links wide.

Which object is wider?

U. Target Numbers (URG p. 24)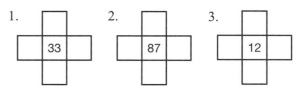

1. 33   2. 87   3. 12

V. Golf Balls or Marbles? (URG p. 24)

Marge's two containers have the same volume and shape. She filled one with golf balls and the other with marbles. Which object do you think there are more of?

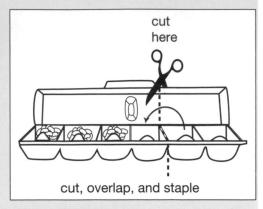

cut
here

cut, overlap, and staple

Figure 9: *Modifying an egg carton from 12 to 10 cups*

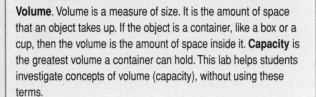

Content Note

Volume. Volume is a measure of size. It is the amount of space that an object takes up. If the object is a container, like a box or a cup, then the volume is the amount of space inside it. **Capacity** is the greatest volume a container can hold. This lab helps students investigate concepts of volume (capacity), without using these terms.

Name _____ Date _____

Full of Beans

Draw

Draw a picture of the lab setup.

Full of Beans   SG • Grade 1 • Unit 9 • Lesson 8   175

Student Guide **- page 175**

Before the Lab

You will need a 2-pound bag of both kidney and large lima beans. Empty the two bags into separate large containers and place them in a central location.

Modify one egg carton for each group. Cut and staple them as shown in Figure 9 so that they have ten sections instead of twelve. Instead of simply cutting off the end, cut each carton in the middle and staple the two parts so they overlap to create an enclosed container that won't leak beans. As an alternative to using egg cartons, draw circles on a piece of paper or use the *Ten Frames* Blackline Master.

Teaching the Lab

Start by demonstrating how to carefully fill a 2-ounce cup with beans. Then, pour the beans on the overhead projector, and ask students to identify the best way to count them. Guide students to the idea of grouping by tens as the counting method to use for the activity. Then, show the modified egg carton and discuss how it can be used for counting. Each carton section can hold a group of ten beans. Explain the steps listed below and have students draw a picture of the procedure before they begin. Students should draw their pictures on the first lab page.

1. Fill a 2-ounce cup to the rim with the smaller beans.
2. Count the beans in the cup by putting groups of ten beans into each egg carton section.
3. Repeat this procedure with the larger beans.

TIMS Tip

In assessing the drawings, look for two cups, the two different sizes of beans, and beans being grouped and counted.

Stipulate that the cup is full when the beans are level with the rim of the cup. Students can check this by laying a piece of paper on top of the cup. This keeps the procedure "fair" when comparing the number of each type of bean required to fill the cups.

Once they have grouped and counted their beans, help groups record their numbers in the group table on the second lab page. Have them write the name of bean or make a tracing of the bean in the first column of the table. After recording their data, ask each group to report their findings.

Draw a number line on the board that includes the range of the class numbers for one type of bean. Record each group's number on the number line, writing the same number again if it represents another group's results. The numbers should be fairly close; if they aren't, you should discuss what could account for large differences. Next, have students help you locate the middle number for the data. If you wish, mention that scientists call this middle number the **median.** To find the median, cross off numbers in highest and lowest pairs until you have only one number left. It is important that you cross off each group's number separately if several groups had the same number. If two numbers are left, the class can choose a number in between as its median and record it on their class data table. Encourage students to use the *100 Chart* to help them order numbers and find numbers "in between," if necessary.

Content Note

Median. The median is a single value used to represent a data set. It is the number exactly in the middle of the data. For example, if five student groups count 41, 42, 42, 44, and 45 beans, the median is 42 beans. If there is an even number of values such as 41, 41, 44, 45 beans, the median is 42.5 beans. For first graders, choosing either 42 or 43 beans is acceptable.

Repeat this procedure for the other type of bean. Students should not be expected to remember the term median at this point; introducing the idea that there is a special name for this number is enough. Ask if anyone remembers the last time they learned about the middle number (*Rolling Along with Links* in Unit 6).

Explain to students that they are going to show the class data on a bar graph. Display the transparency of the graph from the lab pages, and explain what the numbers represent on the vertical axis of the graph and that the two boxes on the horizontal axis represent the columns from the data tables, one for each kind of bean. Work with students to fill in the missing numbers on the vertical axis and write (or draw) the two kinds of beans on the horizontal axis. If your students can do it on their own, have them graph the class data independently; otherwise, demonstrate how to fill in the bar for one kind of bean; then, have students complete the other bar independently.

Conclude by having students revisit the major concepts of the lab in the questions in the Explore section on the last lab page. The questions focus on the idea that more of the smaller beans are required to fill the cup than the larger beans. Use this worksheet to guide a class discussion or give students a chance to work independently. Check students' understanding of the lab concepts by encouraging them to tell why they have more of the smaller bean than they do of the

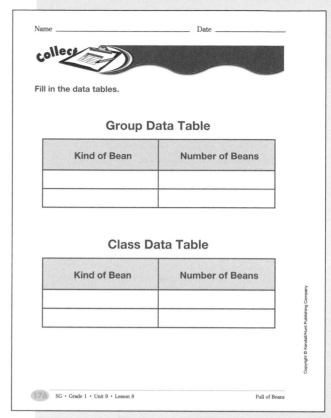

Fill in the data tables.

Group Data Table

Kind of Bean	Number of Beans

Class Data Table

Kind of Bean	Number of Beans

Student Guide - page 176

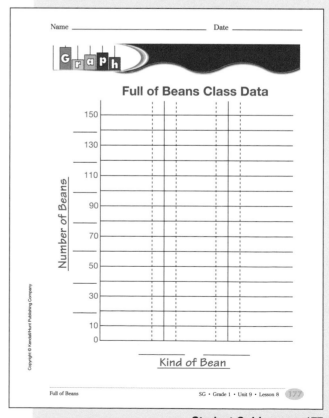

Full of Beans Class Data

Student Guide - page 177

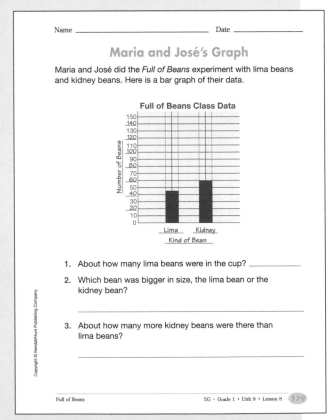

Student Guide - page 178 *(Answers on p. 92)*

Name _____ Date _____

Explore

1. Which kind of bean did your cup hold more of?

   _____

   About how many more? Use your graph to help you.

   _____

2. Which kind of bean was bigger in size?

   _____

3. Will a cup always hold more small beans than big beans? Explain your answer.

   _____

   _____

   _____

4. Work with your partner to answer this question. Then, share with the class how you found your answer.

   If we had a big cup that holds 200 of the small beans, about how many large beans would the cup hold?

   _____

178   SG • Grade 1 • Unit 9 • Lesson 8   Full of Beans

Student Guide - page 179 *(Answers on p. 92)*

Name _____ Date _____

Maria and José's Graph

Maria and José did the *Full of Beans* experiment with lima beans and kidney beans. Here is a bar graph of their data.

Full of Beans Class Data

1. About how many lima beans were in the cup? _____

2. Which bean was bigger in size, the lima bean or the kidney bean?

   _____

3. About how many more kidney beans were there than lima beans?

   _____

Full of Beans   SG • Grade 1 • Unit 9 • Lesson 8   179

---

larger bean. *Question 4* asks students to make a prediction based upon their data. Students' answers to this question can help you assess whether they understand the key volume idea associated with the lab— that fewer large beans would be required. It also can give you an idea of students' perception of the relative size of large numbers. Be sure to discuss this question with the class.

Homework and Practice

DPP item Q builds students' number sense in a game setting. Item R practices skip counting. Item T compares numbers reported in tens and ones. Item U reviews *Target Numbers* from Lesson 5. Item V reviews volume concepts.

Assessment

- Use the *Maria and José's Graph* Assessment Page to assess the skills and concepts presented in the lab.

- Fill a small clear container with identical objects, such as small pasta. Fill another identical container with a group of similar, but larger objects. Label the two jars A and B. Ask students to estimate how many objects are in each of the two containers. Estimates should indicate students' understanding that fewer of the larger objects will fit in the container. Ask them to report their estimates and reasoning in their journals.

Journal Prompt

I think there are _____ objects in jar A and _____ objects in jar B. I think I'm right because . . .

- Use DPP item S to assess students' abilities to place numbers in intervals.

- Use the *Observational Assessment Record* to document students' abilities to make and interpret bar graphs and to use data to solve problems involving volume.

- Transfer appropriate documentation from the Unit 9 *Observational Assessment Record* to students' *Individual Assessment Record Sheets*.

Extension

Use the data from the lab to create various arithmetic problems for students to solve.

At a Glance

Math Facts Strategies and Daily Practice and Problems

DPP items Q–V develop number sense.

Teaching the Lab

1. Discuss the problem and demonstrate the lab procedure.
2. Students draw a picture showing the materials and the process on the first *Full of Beans* Lab Page.
3. Students take a 2-ounce sample of small beans and count them by grouping into tens and ones using a modified egg carton. They repeat the process for large beans.
4. Students collect data for the large and small beans and record their numbers in a data table.
5. Students find the median value of the class data for each kind of bean.
6. Students draw a bar graph for their data.
7. Students complete the questions on the *Full of Beans* Lab Pages.

Assessment

1. Use the *Maria and José's Graph* Assessment Page.
2. Fill a small container with a group of objects and another identical container with a group of larger objects. Label one jar A and the other B. Ask students to estimate how many objects are in each container and record their estimates and reasoning in their journals.
3. Use DPP item S as a short assessment.
4. Use Assessment Indicators A5 and A6 and the *Observational Assessment Record* to document students' abilities to make and interpret bar graphs and to use data to solve problems involving volume.
5. Transfer appropriate documentation from the Unit 9 *Observational Assessment Record* to students' *Individual Assessment Record Sheets.*

Extension

Use the data table from the lab to create arithmetic problems.

Answer Key is on page 92.

Notes:

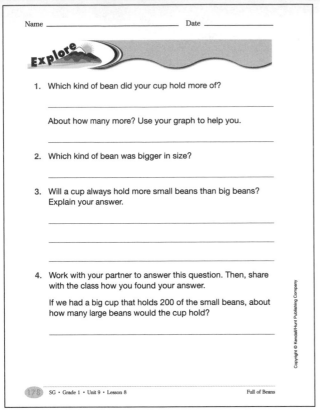

Student Guide - page 178

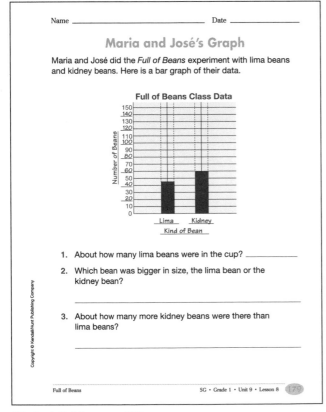

Student Guide - page 179

Student Guide (p. 178)

Full of Beans

Pictures, data tables, and graphs will vary.
Answers will vary based on data collected.*

Student Guide (p. 179)

Maria and José's Graph

1. About 45

2. Lima

3. 15 beans

*Answers and/or discussion are included in the Lesson Guide.

Glossary

This glossary provides definitions of key vocabulary terms in the Grade 1 lessons. Locations of key vocabulary terms in the curriculum are included with each definition. Components Key: URG = *Unit Resource Guide* and SG = *Student Guide*.

A

Approximate (URG Unit 12)
1. (adjective) a number that is close to the desired number
2. (verb) to estimate

Area (URG Unit 10; SG Unit 12)
The amount of space that a shape covers. Area is measured in square units.

B

C

Capacity (URG Unit 9)
1. The volume of the inside of a container.
2. The largest volume a container can hold.

Circle (URG Unit 2)
A curve that is made up of all the points that are the same distance from one point, the center.

Circumference (URG Unit 15)
The distance around a circle.

Coordinates (URG Unit 19)
(In the plane) Two numbers that specify the location of a point on a flat surface relative to a reference point called the origin. The two numbers are the distances from the point to two perpendicular lines called axes.

Counting All (URG Unit 1)
A strategy for adding in which students start at one and count until the total is reached.

Counting Back (URG Unit 8)
A method of subtraction that involves counting from the larger number to the smaller one. For example, to find 8 − 5 the student counts 7, 6, 5 which is 3 less.

Counting On (URG Unit 1 & Unit 4)
A strategy for adding two numbers in which students start with one of the numbers and then count until the total is reached. For example, to count 6 + 3, begin with 6 and count three more, 7, 8, 9.

Counting Up (URG Unit 8)
A method of subtraction that involves counting from the smaller number to the larger one. For example, to find 8 − 5 the student counts 6, 7, 8 which is 3 more.

Cube (URG Unit 12 & Unit 15)
A solid with six congruent square faces.

Cubic Units (URG Unit 12)
A unit for measuring volume—a cube that measures one unit along each edge. For example, cubic centimeters and cubic inches.

cubic centimeter

Cylinder (URG Unit 15)
A three-dimensional figure with two parallel congruent circles as bases (top and bottom) and a curved side that is the union of parallel lines connecting corresponding points on the circles.

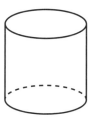

D

Data Table (URG Unit 3)
A tool for recording and organizing data on paper or on a computer.

Name	Age

Division by Measuring Out (URG Unit 14)

A type of division problem in which the number in each group is known and the unknown is the number of groups. For example, twenty students are divided into teams of four students each. How many teams are there? (20 students ÷ 4 students per team = 5 teams) This type of division is also known as measurement division.

Division by Sharing (URG Unit 14)

A type of division problem in which the number of groups is known and the unknown is the number in each group. For example, twenty students are divided into five teams. How many students are on each team? (20 students ÷ 5 teams = 4 students per team) This type of division is also known as partitive division.

E

Edge (URG Unit 15)

A line segment where two faces of a three-dimensional figure meet.

Equivalent Fractions (URG Unit 18)

Two fractions are equivalent if they represent the same part of the whole. For example, if a class has 8 boys and 8 girls, we can say $\frac{8}{16}$ of the students are girls or $\frac{1}{2}$ of the students are girls.

Even Number (URG Unit 4 & Unit 13)

Numbers that are doubles. The numbers 0, 2, 4, 6, 8, 10, etc. are even. The number 28 is even because it is 14 + 14.

F

Face (URG Unit 12 & Unit 15)

A flat side of a three-dimensional figure.

Fixed Variables (URG Unit 2, Unit 6 & Unit 11)

Variables in an experiment that are held constant or not changed. These variables are often called controlled variables.

G

H

Hexagon (URG Unit 2)

A six-sided polygon.

I

J

K

L

Length (URG Unit 6 & Unit 10)

1. The distance along a line or curve from one point to another. Distance can be measured with a ruler or tape measure.
2. The distance from one "end" to another of a two- or three-dimensional figure. For example, the length of a rectangle usually refers to the length of the longer side.

Line

A set of points that form a straight path extending infinitely in two directions.

Line Symmetry (URG Unit 7 & Unit 18)

A figure has line symmetry if it can be folded along a line so that the two halves match exactly.

Line of Symmetry (URG Unit 7 & Unit 18)

A line such that if a figure is folded along the line, then one half of the figure matches the other.

M

Making a Ten (URG Unit 13)

A strategy for adding and subtracting that takes advantage of students' knowledge of partitions of ten. For example, a student might find 8 + 4 by breaking the 4 into 2 + 2 and then using a knowledge of sums that add to ten.

$$8 + 4 =$$
$$8 + 2 + 2 =$$
$$10 + 2 = 12$$

Median (URG Unit 6 & Unit 9)

The number "in the middle" of a set of data. If there is an odd number of data, it is the number in the middle when the numbers are arranged in order. So the median of {1, 2, 14, 15, 28, 29, 30} is 15. If there is an even number of data, it is the number halfway between the two middle numbers. The median of {1, 2, 14, 15, 28, 29} is $14\frac{1}{2}$.

Mr. Origin (URG Unit 19)

A plastic figure used to help childen learn about direction and distance.

N

Near Double (URG Unit 13)

A derived addition or subtraction fact found by using doubles. For example, 3 + 4 = 7 follows from the fact that 3 + 3 = 6.

Number Sentence (URG Unit 3 & Unit 4)

A number sentence uses numbers and symbols instead of words to describe a problem. For example, a number sentence for the problem "5 birds landed on a branch. Two more birds also landed on the branch. How many birds are on the branch?" is 5 + 2 = 7.

O

Odd Number (URG Unit 4)
A number that is not even. The odd numbers are 1, 3, 5, 7, 9, and so on.

Origin (URG Unit 19)
A reference point for a coordinate system. If the coordinate system is a line, we can determine the location of an object on the line by the number of units it is to the right or the left of the origin.

P

Part (URG Unit 4)
One of the addends in part-part-whole addition problems.

Pattern Unit (URG Unit 7)
The portion of a pattern that is repeated. For example, AAB is the pattern unit in the pattern AABAABAAB.

Perimeter (URG Unit 6; SG Unit 12)
The distance around a two-dimensional shape.

Polygon
A closed, connected plane figure consisting of line segments, with exactly two segments meeting at each end point.

Polygons   Not Polygons

Prediction (URG Unit 5)
Using a sample to predict what is likely to occur in the population.

Prism (URG Unit 15)
A solid that has two congruent and parallel bases. The remaining faces (sides) are parallelograms. A rectangular prism has bases that are rectangles. A box is a common object that is shaped like a rectangular prism.

Q

Quadrilateral
A polygon with four sides.

R

Rectangle (URG Unit 2)
A quadrilateral with four right angles.

Rhombus (URG Unit 2)
A quadrilateral with four sides of equal length.

Rotational Symmetry (URG Unit 7)

Rotational Symmetry (URG Unit 7)
A figure has rotational (or turn) symmetry if there is a point on the figure and a rotation of less than 360° about that point so that it "fits" on itself. For example, a square has a turn symmetry of $\frac{1}{4}$ turn (or 90°) about its center.

S

Sample (URG Unit 5)
Some of the items from a whole group.

Sphere (URG Unit 15)
A three-dimensional figure that is made up of points that are the same distance from one point, the center. A basketball is a common object shaped like a sphere.

Square (URG Unit 2)
A polygon with four equal sides and four right angles.

Symmetry (URG Unit 18)
(See Line Symmetry, Line of Symmetry, and Rotational Symmetry.)

T

Three-dimensional Shapes (URG Unit 15)
A figure in space that has length, width, and height.

TIMS Laboratory Method (URG Unit 5)
A method that students use to organize experiments and investigations. It involves four components: draw, collect, graph, and explore. It is a way to help students learn about the scientific method. TIMS is an acronym for Teaching Integrated Mathematics and Science.

Trapezoid (URG Unit 2)
A quadrilateral with exactly one pair of parallel sides.

Trial (URG Unit 6)
One attempt in an experiment.

Triangle (URG Unit 2)
A polygon with three sides.

Turn Symmetry
(See Rotational Symmetry.)

U

Using Doubles (URG Unit 13)
A strategy for adding and subtracting which uses derived facts from known doubles. For example, students use 7 + 7 = 14 to find that 7 + 8 is one more or 15.

Using Ten (URG Unit 13)
A strategy for adding which uses reasoning from known facts. For example, students use 3 + 7 = 10 to find that 4 + 7 is one more or 11.

V

Variable (URG Unit 2 & Unit 11)
A variable is something that varies or changes in an experiment.

Volume (URG Unit 9 & Unit 12;
   SG Unit 12)
1. The amount of space an object takes up.
2. The amount of space inside a container.

W

Whole (URG Unit 4)
The sum in part-part-whole addition problems.

X

Y

Z